CONFIDENCE
IN THE
LIVING
GOD

Published by
The Bible Reading Fellowship
15 The Chambers, Vineyard
Abingdon OX14 3FE
United Kingdom
Tel: +44 (0)1865 319700
Email: enquiries@brf.org.uk
Website: www.brf.org.uk

ISBN 978 0 85746 482 8
First published 2009
This edition 2016
10 9 8 7 6 5 4 3 2 1 0
All rights reserved

Acknowledgements

Unless otherwise stated, scripture quotations taken from the Holy Bible, Today's New International Version, copyright © 2004 by International Bible Society, and are used by permission of Hodder & Stoughton Publishers, a division of Hodder Headline Ltd. All rights reserved. 'TNIV' is a registered trademark of International Bible Society.

Scripture quotations taken from the Holy Bible, New International Version, copyright © 1973, 1978, 1984 by International Bible Society, are used by permission of Hodder & Stoughton Publishers, a division of Hodder Headline Ltd. All rights reserved. 'NIV' is a registered trademark of International Bible Society. UK trademark number 1448790.

Scripture quotations taken from the Revised Standard Version of the Bible, copyright © 1946, 1952, 1971 by the Division of Christian Education of the National Council of the Churches of Christ in the United States of America, are used by permission. All rights reserved.

Cover photo: © Thinkstock

Every effort has been made to trace and contact copyright owners for material used in this resource. We apologise for any inadvertent omissions or errors, and would ask those concerned to contact us so that full acknowledgement can be made in the future.

A catalogue record for this book is available from the British Library

Printed and bound by CPI Group (UK) Ltd, Croydon CR0 4YY

CONFIDENCE
IN THE
LIVING
GOD

David & Goliath revisited

ANDREW WATSON

Contents

— Foreword —

The post-war Church of England appeared to be a Goliath bestriding the national stage in a way that could not be ignored. In a period of reconstruction, within the living memory of many of today's church attenders, Sunday schools were thronged and an abundance of curates refreshed the parochial ministry.

The poet Philip Larkin thought that 1963 was the watershed year when 'sexual intercourse was invented' but the student turbulence of 1968 was the most obvious sign of a social and psycho-spiritual revolution. Now the children of that revolution rule in most Western countries where it really counts in education and the media.

The church felt perhaps too much at home in the old world and has been wandering amazed and bewildered during the near 50 years since 1968. With honourable exceptions like the Faith in the City campaign, the church at a national level has spent its time fussing with in-house preoccupations and elaborating defensive bureaucracy.

During those years, however, the Holy Spirit has been at work in the most surprising places, rebuilding confidence in a church that has lost its Goliath-like pretensions and may now, in consequence, be prepared to listen to the example of the young David.

Andrew Watson's book is constructed around the story of the contest between David and Goliath in the first book of Samuel. Instead of proceeding by abstractions, the author probes the story for spiritually significant pointers to the nature and practice of Christian confidence.

There is nothing here of the breezy optimism which is so

often the prelude to disillusionment. Too often, those who are superficially upbeat in the first part of their ministry are condemned to a spiritual hangover in its latter stages. True Christian confidence yokes the confidence that Christ is God's unshakeable intention for the future of the human race with a refusal to indulge in any wishful thinking or denial of the evidence that the contemporary community of believers is, in the eyes of the world, very weak.

The book also contains useful reflections on the character of Christian leadership, which involves subjecting our own egotistical agenda to the greater ambition of building, together with others, an embodied hope, larger and longer lasting than ourselves. There are very helpful lessons about the distinction to be drawn between a down-to-earth personal humility and an unattractive self-absorption, together with the imperative not to yield to lethargy. Confidence also grows with training in the virtues and a disciplined personal life.

Andrew Watson has tested these ideas in a number of demanding spheres of parish ministry and the book is illuminated by examples from his own pastoral experience. Now, as a bishop, he has been called to help the church choose a pathway through the next 50 years in which, having been parted from the pretensions of Goliath, it has a possibility of recovering David's confidence in the living God.

+ Richard Londin

— Introduction —

The Call to Confidence

In the mid-1980s I was boarding a train, and as I stepped into the carriage I saw an African bishop sitting there reading a book. I guessed he was African by the colour of his skin. I guessed he was a bishop by the colour of his shirt. So I promptly sat down on the seat beside him and greeted him, at which point he introduced himself as Festo Kivengere.

I knew the name of Festo Kivengere even then—a man of outstanding courage and integrity who'd lived through the most brutal years of Uganda's recent history and had responded by writing a remarkable book entitled *I Love Idi Amin*. A gifted evangelist, a close friend of Billy Graham, someone whose ministry was founded on three great gospel cornerstones—forgiveness, reconciliation and proclamation—there were few people in the world whom I would rather have met than Bishop Festo. And as the conversation continued, so I was quietly praising God for engineering this meeting with one of the spiritual greats.

Then the bishop started to share the gospel. I don't remember his opening gambit, but there was no question that *he* was looking forward to a meeting, at the end of which his travelling companion—that was me—would be giving his life to Christ in repentance and faith, perhaps followed by a chilly baptism on arrival. It was at that point that I thought I'd better come clean, and tell him that I was already a Christian and preparing for ordained ministry. It was such a delight and a privilege, I continued, to meet a man whom I'd heard so much about.

'You're already a Christian?' repeated Bishop Festo.

'Yes,' I replied.

'Well, what are you doing sitting next to a bishop?' he responded. 'It's no wonder that the church is in decline in your country if Christians sit next to Christians in train compartments. Find someone who isn't a Christian, and tell them about Jesus!' And so (rather shamefacedly) I left my place beside the bishop, found a different seat, and, much to my surprise, struck up a conversation with a lapsed Catholic which was remarkably fruitful and honest!

And as I later reflected on that train journey, I felt suitably chastised, but also encouraged, challenged and freshly persuaded of the need for me personally, and much of the church of which I am a part, to rediscover a genuine, unabashed confidence in the living God and the gospel of Christ. Not a confidence in the schemes and strategies and evangelistic programmes which I would shortly be starting to implement; not some foolish, triumphalistic confidence which was blind to the fallenness of the world outside me (and still more blind to the fallenness of the world within); but a confidence in God himself, in his love, his power, his calling, and his ability to mould even me into something useful for his kingdom purposes here on earth.

'God did not give us a spirit of timidity', as the mighty Paul wrote to Timothy, his youthful protégé, 'but a spirit of power, of love and of self-discipline' (2 Timothy 1:7, NIV); and my rather abrupt encounter with the mighty Festo effectively communicated just the same message 2000 years on.

Confidence unwrapped

It is not just courageous bishops or timid ordinands who might usefully reflect on the theme of confidence. In a very real sense it is confidence which lies at the very heart of the market economy, confidence which determines the success or failure of every human institution, and confidence which makes the lives of individuals either positive and resilient or painful and resigned. Confidence in the leadership and vision of a school, business or political party is a central factor in the rise or fall of the entire enterprise. Confidence in the FTSE index and the housing and money markets wholly dictates the monetary value of companies and property, and even the monetary value of money itself! Confidence in an interview plays a major, often decisive, part in the wording of the letter which arrives on the doormat a few days later. Confidence in the sporting arena separates the gold medallists from the also-rans.

What, though, does the word 'confidence' really mean, and how do we recognise it in an individual or an institution?

The Latin from which our English word is derived (*con fide*) means 'with faith', and suggests that confident people both have faith in themselves (or perhaps in their god) and inspire the faith of others: hence their frequent successes in the interview room and around the boardroom table. That faith may well be misplaced or misguided: it is quite possible for individuals or institutions to be confident and incompetent, or even confident and corrupt. That faith may be self-serving and off-putting. But where combined with ability, integrity and modesty, there is something about this gift of confidence which is both attractive and inspiring. Confident people have a sureness of step, whatever the complexities of modern-day living. Confident institutions know where they're going, whatever the challenges they encounter along the way.

The biblical languages add something to this understanding. The root of the Hebrew word most often translated 'confidence' (*beTach*) has the sense of being open, of having nothing to hide (so stressing the integrity theme), while two Greek words *parrhesia* and *pepoithesis* convey a sense of assurance, trust and boldness. A third Greek word, *hupostasis*, means literally something 'set under' something else, hence a foundation. When the author of the letter to the Hebrews writes, 'We have come to share in Christ if we hold firmly till the end the confidence we had at first' (3:14, NIV), his use of the word *hupostasis* suggests that the Church's original confidence in Christ is foundational, and is therefore able to endure the toughest of challenges and temptations.

Building on such a foundation doesn't preclude us from placing a proper confidence in our nearest and dearest, of course: the husband of the exemplary wife in Proverbs 31 'has full confidence in her and lacks nothing of value' (v. 11), while Paul, writing to the troublesome church at Corinth, emphasises (perhaps a little too often!) how he has 'complete confidence' in them (for example, 2 Corinthians 7:16). But when it comes to the very underpinning of our lives—our deepest security as human beings—there is no question that God alone is to be trusted, and we are to accept no cheap imitations.

So where does that leave self-confidence in a biblical understanding? Is this attribute—which is generally what people mean when they use the 'c' word of a friend or colleague—a virtue or a vice when it comes to the Christian believer?

At first sight it would appear that confidence in God

excludes a confidence in ourselves, that the two simply cannot coexist. In Philippians 3, after all, Paul writes of the dangers of putting 'confidence in the flesh', and emphatically considers all his worldly advantages as so much 'garbage' compared with the 'surpassing worth of knowing Christ Jesus my Lord' (v. 8). Christian doctrine relating to sin, humility and self-denial hardly sits easily with secular teaching on confidence and self-esteem; and as a result many Christians steer clear of the language of self-confidence, regularly acknowledging the dangers of living 'in my own strength' and stressing (with the prophet Isaiah) that all their righteous acts are like 'filthy rags' (64:6).

There is another side to this argument, though—one that allows for the possibility that confidence in God and a proper self-confidence are more closely related than we sometimes think. A useful analogy might perhaps be drawn with the question of whether our love for God diminishes or excludes all other loves: for while it's true that Jesus uses a graphic Jewish idiom to emphasise that nothing should compete with our primary relationship with him (Luke 14:26), the call to 'love one another' (and even the assumption that we love ourselves: Matthew 22:38–39) could hardly be stronger in the Gospels or the New Testament as a whole. Might there, then, be a parallel situation when it comes to confidence, a sense in which our confidence in God (and in the gifts, abilities and life experiences with which he has entrusted us) can enhance, not eclipse, a proper confidence in ourselves? It is an intriguing question, and one to which we will return later in the book.

Self-confidence is one conundrum, but another is the practical question of how our confidence in God equips us for the challenges of our day-to-day living. We have already referred to the Greek word *hupostasis*, which carries the sense of something foundational; but while there is real value in viewing our lives as a building project, a more natural metaphor is arguably that of a journey—a 'pilgrim's progress' from the City of Destruction to the Celestial City via the Wicket Gate, the King's Highway, the Hill of Difficulty and Doubting Castle.[2]

The steady erection of a building, brick by brick, has something ordered and predictable about it, but the journey throws up challenges that are frequently unasked for and unexpected. For the recipients of the letter to the Hebrews, the largest cloud on the horizon was the growing threat of persecution; for us it may be the demands of a seemingly intractable work situation, the strains of a difficult marriage, the stresses of parenting a stubborn toddler or teenager, or a host of anxieties relating to unemployment, money, health or the future. Against such a backdrop we need the foundations, but we also need the capacity to improvise, to think on our feet, to be 'life confident'—the ability, in a sense, to treat confidence as a verb (something we do) as much as a noun (something we have).

It is perhaps that sense of confidence as a verb which leads many to be drawn more to the story of courageous individuals than to the abstract reflections of the philosopher or theologian: for if our lives are a spiritual journey (charting one particular 'pilgrim's progress'), it is instructive to look at the progress of others and to draw parallels between their experiences and our own. There is a danger in this approach, of course: if we are to search for the *foundations* of our confidence as Christian believers, we are much more likely to find them in Paul's letter to the Romans than in the story of a Moses or a Mother Teresa.[3] But there is also a freshness and immediacy about the accounts of men and women responding to God, often in the toughest and most challenging of circumstances; and the growing influence of so-called 'narrative theology'—a theology based on the storyline of scripture more than its great doctrinal formulations—is a constructive response to the human need for such stories, as well as a positive attempt to do justice to a 'living God' whose story intersects with our own.[4]

Having had a first exploration of our theme of confidence, then, it is time to introduce the narrative around which this book is to be centred: the story of David and Goliath in 1 Samuel 17.

The giant and the shepherd boy

Of all the stories in the Old Testament there are few that are widely known and recognised. A cartoonist or sketch-writer might safely use the image of Adam and Eve in the garden (acknowledging that their story retains some cultural resonance), while Noah's Ark would be their next clear port of call. The history of Abraham, Isaac and Jacob would be entirely bypassed, while Joseph would probably get a look-in, thanks to the efforts of Messrs Rice and Lloyd Webber and the startling nature of his Technicolor Dreamcoat.[5] The parting of the Red Sea might just detain our cartoonist for a moment, but otherwise the accounts of Moses, Joshua, the judges and the kings would largely go unnoticed. Later in the Old Testament, only Daniel in the lions' den and Jonah in his fish's belly might figure briefly, though even their memory is fading from the public consciousness.

The one additional story we must add to the list is that of David and Goliath: for the description of their mismatched encounter in the first book of Samuel has remained something of a cultural icon through the ages, attracting painters, sculptors, musicians and poets, and acting as an almost clichéd metaphor for the hopes of the underdog in the context of political contests, business takeovers and football fixtures. In the days of the Renaissance, the city of Florence adopted young David as their patron saint, and Michelangelo's famous statue came to personify the spirit of the new republic which had successfully chased the Medici from the city ten years earlier. In more recent times the David and Goliath story has regularly been evoked to describe the heroic struggles against apartheid in South Africa and communism in the former Soviet Union, '[embodying] the hopes of all persons when they are faced with overwhelming and evil power that there is a way to overcome that power and win the future'.[6]

Children love the story of David and Goliath both for its spirit of courage and adventure, and, some would argue, 'because they also live in a world of oppressive giants'.[7] Orators love the story because of its potential to stiffen the sinews and stir the soul. Is the church embattled, taking the role of David against the well-armed forces of a secular fundamentalism? Or are the secularists themselves embattled, fighting for truth and freedom against the overweening power of superstition and *religious* fundamentalism? In many a debate the success of the final outcome will depend on the skill with which each side positions themselves as a David and their opponent as a Goliath.

It is possible, of course, to know the broad outlines of a story without having read it, but for those who choose to engage with 1 Samuel 17 itself there is a treat in store. The chapter is the most detailed of all the David stories, and, in the words of Bruce C. Birch, is 'as close as one can come in the Hebrew Bible to an epic style of storytelling—rich and explicit detail, extensive use of vivid dialogue, strong characterisation and interaction of characters'.[8] The writer of the books of Samuel is particularly strong in communicating real people, not cardboard cut-outs, a gift which extends to the minor characters in the drama (Hannah, Elkanah, Eli, Jonathan) as much as to the essential trio of Samuel, Saul and David (or perhaps more accurately, the essential quartet of Samuel, Saul, David and God); and that strength is displayed in this chapter, with Saul, David and Eliab brilliantly portrayed, and only Goliath perhaps lacking something in psychological depth (if not in physical bulk!).

Walter Brueggemann, a scholar who has written extensively on the Samuel stories,[9] divides his treatment of 1 Samuel into three parts: the Rise of Samuel (chapters 1—7), the Rule of Saul (chapters 8—15), and the Rise of David (chapter 16 through to 2 Samuel 5:10); and clearly the defeat of Goliath (played out in front of a massive audience and culminating in a chart-topping song in David's honour: see 1 Samuel 18:7) was a key step in the shepherd boy's rise to the throne. David is as central to the books of Samuel as Jesus is to the Gospels, with even the early chapters of 1 Samuel simply providing the backdrop for David's arrival on the scene; and like the Gospel writers, the author of the books of Samuel is 'deeply and endlessly fascinated'[10] with the central character in the drama that unfolds.

There is just one major difficulty in choosing this story as the base camp for any exploration of the theme of confidence: it includes the account of a death and beheading, alongside a massacre which left Philistine bodies 'strewn along the Shaaraim road to Gath and Ekron' (1 Samuel

17:52). In the context of events in modern-day Israel—and set against the rise of a particularly ferocious brand of Islamic fundamentalism—it might be thought unwise to choose a text which is so uncompromising in its descriptions of physical violence, simply playing into the hands of a Richard Dawkins, say, or a Christopher Hitchens.[11] Yet while ours is not to judge the justness of an ancient war between the Israelites and the Philistines, it is important to stress from the outset that the Christian gospel itself is not to be spread by anything other than peaceful means. Even David the shepherd boy might have dimly glimpsed that truth in his affirmation that 'it is not by sword or spear that the Lord saves' (1 Samuel 17:47), but it would be 'great David's greater Son'[12] who would turn that rhetoric into reality, consistently rejecting the violent approach of the Zealots of his day and gloriously fulfilling Isaiah's prophecy (9:6) of the arrival of a 'Prince of Peace'.

The way ahead

My approach in the following chapters is, I hope, an uncomplicated one: for as an amateur but enthusiastic birdwatcher, I plan to look at just one chapter of scripture through a pair of long-range binoculars.

The right eye[13] will constantly be focused on the storyline itself—on helping us to understand the narrative, to set it in context and to enjoy the brilliance of the storyteller's art. Although I will allude to various textual difficulties and to the odd apparent contradiction along the way, my priority will be to centre on the story as it is, rather than to speculate on how it came to be there. Equally significant, though, will be the view of the left eye, with its focus on the theme of confidence, and the application and relevance of this story for today.

In general the storyline will direct the shape of this book,[14] but that doesn't rule out some kind of structure in the confidence discussions. Indeed, the story itself explores so many confidence themes that it seems ideally suited to this 'binocular' treatment.

It would be possible, of course, to study the narrative of David and Goliath as an academic text, with no thought to its application or ongoing relevance. It would equally be possible to write a book about 'confidence in the living God' with little or no reference to 1 Samuel at all. But to look through both lenses of a pair of binoculars (provided they are properly focused and in line with one another) brings greater depth and definition than to look through one alone; and my hope and prayer is that this book will draw new wisdom and insight from this most familiar of stories so as to release faith, zeal, passion and confidence within God's people, for the blessing of his world and the glory of his name.

— 1 —

Building Confident Foundations: Introducing the Philistines

History repeats itself.
Has to.
Nobody listens.[1]

It's one of Steve Turner's more succinct poems, but it still packs a punch. For the reality is that humankind is often extraordinarily bad at learning from history, so consigning itself to a tedious repetition of the same mistakes time and time again. Individuals, families, churches, communities, whole nations fall prey to this tendency. Even in successful organisations, a laudable emphasis on vision for the future all too often replaces (rather than supplements) an accompanying emphasis on reflection on the past. And the result is this: that precisely those lessons that we should be squirrelling away, so developing a deposit of wisdom and godly confidence within us, are instead strewn behind us like so much litter as we continue our headlong rush onwards and (all too rarely) upwards.

For a number of years I was privileged to live near a particularly beautiful stretch of the River Thames, and my morning walks beside the river were frequently punctuated by the sound of a cox bellowing orders to a boatful of rowers. The cox could see straight ahead, and guide the boat in the right direction, yet the power came from the oarsmen facing the opposite way; and there's something of that interplay between cox and oarsmen—between the composite need for looking forwards and reflecting backwards—which seems fundamental to vigorous, purposeful living.[2]

No Future Without Forgiveness is the title of Desmond Tutu's reflections on the Truth and Reconciliation Commission in South Africa,[3] and its second chapter movingly describes both the humiliation of apartheid and the complex discussions which led to the Commission's formation after the glorious elections of April 1994. On the one hand there were many who argued for the approach of the Nuremberg Trials, letting those who had perpetrated the worst atrocities of the apartheid era 'run the gauntlet of the normal judicial process'. On the other, there were some who suggested that the blanket amnesty secured by General Pinochet in Chile was the only practicable model, effectively whitewashing decades of human rights abuses. While the Nuremberg approach was quickly rejected, the notion that South Africa should embrace a kind of national amnesia was seen as still more repugnant, turning those who had been 'cruelly silenced for so long' into 'anonymous, marginalised victims'. The approach of the Commission—which granted an amnesty to individuals in exchange for a full disclosure of what they had done—proved both realistic and healing, facing up to the past while avoiding the danger of individual vendettas or a partial 'victor's justice'.

More personally, I was recently involved in a conversation with a newly engaged couple prior to their marriage. Both were Christians, both were in their late 40s, and one had been married before. At some point in the conversation I raised the issue of the previous marriage, and was greatly surprised at the reaction it provoked. 'We've never talked about that,' said the prospective husband. 'We really don't think it would be helpful.' 'No,' continued the prospective wife, 'it feels like it happened in a different life.' It's not that I was expecting a blow-by-blow account of the earlier relationship, but the idea that such a key event should somehow have become a no-go area between them, consigned to some fictitious 'different life', hardly inspired a sense of confidence in the stability of their future marriage.[4]

And so we turn to the first few verses in the story of David and Goliath, and to the question of what the Israelites might have learnt, had they taken the time and trouble to reflect on their previous dealings with their Philistine opponents.

Facing backwards

Now the Philistines gathered their forces for war and assembled at Sokoh in Judah. They pitched camp at Ephes Dammim, between Sokoh and Azekah. Saul and the Israelites assembled and camped in the Valley of Elah and drew up their battle line to meet the Philistines. The Philistines occupied one hill and the Israelites another, with the valley between them.
1 SAMUEL 17:1–3

It's a prosaic start to an exciting story, locating the source of the future battle around ten miles west of the little town of Bethlehem, as the Philistines sought to expand their territory at Israel's expense. But it suggests a fairly leisurely process of assembling and setting up camp, with no immediate sense of hurry or panic: an ideal opportunity for Saul, we might think, to provide the kind of reflective and inspirational leadership required for the challenges that lay ahead.

Israel had encountered the Philistines on many previous

occasions, and each of those meetings (the good, the bad and the disastrous) had provided considerable food for thought for all who were willing to 'read, mark, learn and inwardly digest' them.[5] The ground on which the battle was to be fought had its own memories too, memories of a stunning Israelite victory, as we will later discover. While they gathered their forces and sat around their campfires, then, Saul and his men might usefully have looked to the past and asked some searching questions about the Philistines and the history of their previous encounters. Unfortunately the paralysis of the Israelite army that we read of later in the chapter suggests that the opportunity was lost, and no such reflection took place.

Who were the Philistines?

The Philistines generally receive a distinctly bad press. In the Bible they play the role of Israel's inveterate enemies, more famous and formidable than the Canaanites, the Hittites, the Amorites, the Perizzites, the Hivites and the Jebusites put together;[6] while through history—and especially in the past 200 years—their name has been associated with all that is mercenary, banal and lowbrow. 'He's a right Philistine!' as we might put it.

In the 1860s Matthew Arnold championed high culture as opposed to the popular tastes of the 'philistines' of his day. Some years before, the composer Robert Schumann had brought together his so-called 'League of David', whose defence of the classical tradition, he felt, was being assaulted by the banality of Rossini and the 'downright amateurism' of Richard Wagner.[7] To Schumann, David was first and foremost a poet and musician, 'Israel's singer of songs' (2

Samuel 23:1, NIV), and his defeat of the Philistines more a
cultural statement than a military victory.[8]

In reality, though, the Philistines of David's day were
people of real discernment and sophistication. Four out of
five of their major strongholds—Ashkelon, Ashdod, Gath and
Ekron—have now been excavated,[9] revealing a formidable
combination of superior technology, military might and
artistic ingenuity. The painstaking studies of archaeologists
like Neal Bierling,[10] who worked on the Ekron site, have
established significant links between the Philistines and the
worlds of Mycenae, Crete and Troy; and while the Philistine
script has still to be fully deciphered, there is no question
that the Philistines were considerably more advanced
technologically (if not theologically) than their Israelite
neighbours.

Where did the Philistines come from? It seems that they
were among the so-called Sea Peoples who were displaced
during the political upheavals around the Aegean during
the 13th century BC and who responded by launching two
attacks on Egypt. The second of these was during the reign
of the Pharaoh Ramesses III, with contemporary Egyptian
records apparently naming the Philistines among other
groups involved in the planned invasion; and Ramesses later
boasted of how he had defeated the People of the Sea and
forced them to settle in citadels on Canaan's southern sea
coast in what we call Palestine (itself a name derived from
the word for 'Philistine') or Israel.

Artistically the Philistines specialised in a unique form
of pottery, with a white background and red and black
decorations in the forms of birds, fish and geometric shapes.
Agriculturally they took full advantage of the excellent
conditions for growing olive trees, with one excavation

containing the remains of more than a hundred olive presses. In terms of religion they ignored the Greek gods and goddesses, and embraced instead the worship of Baal, Asherah, Dagon and Mot, the pantheon of the Canaanites among whom they lived. Technologically they mastered the art of ironwork, building kilns capable of reaching the metal's melting point of 1530°C. Iron weapons could be produced at lower temperatures, but only the hotter kilns would produce a metal which was stronger and more durable than the bronze weaponry of their neighbours.

Given what we now know of the Philistines, then, there is a sense in which the story of David and Goliath represents the collision of two worlds: the Greek world of Homer's *The Iliad*[11] and the Hebrew world of the Bible, with a smattering of Canaanite mythology thrown in for good measure. The very idea of a duel between champions, alongside the vivid description of Goliath's armour and his blood-curdling taunts, has far more in common with the world of *The Iliad* than with that of ancient Israel. But the fierce faith of David in Yahweh, in the 'living God', is far removed from the scheming world of the gods and goddesses in Homer's epic. Indeed it is the clash of these cultures, not simply the details of the fight itself or its place in David's rise to kingship, which makes this story so gripping.

Four lessons from history

What were the lessons that Saul and the Israelites might have learnt as they gathered for war and camped together in the Valley of Elah?

Lesson one was that the Philistines were formidable opponents. In terms of their ambitions, they already had parts of Israel's territory surrounded, and seemed intent on continued expansion into the very heart of the 'promised land'.[12] In terms of their numbers, they'd recently managed to assemble 3000 chariots, 6000 charioteers and (allowing for a little poetic licence) 'soldiers as numerous as the sand on the seashore' (1 Samuel 13:5). In terms of their firepower, the humiliating sight of the Israelites having to go to Philistine blacksmiths to have their ploughshares, mattocks, axes and sickles sharpened (13:20) acted as a stark reminder of the military impotence of the Israelite forces, when compared to the well-armed Philistine militia. On a day when Saul's son Jonathan remarkably triumphed at the battle of Michmash, we are told that only he and King Saul had a sword or spear in their hands (13:22). The rest of the Israelites were presumably fighting with axes and sickles—hardly an impressive sight when compared with the forged iron weaponry of their opponents.

Lesson two, though, was that the Philistines were not invincible. For one thing, several Israelite leaders had scored notable victories over them—the little-known judge Shamgah, for example, who 'struck down six hundred Philistines with an ox-goad' (Judges 3:31); the better-known judge Samson, whose call to 'begin the deliverance of Israel from the hands of the Philistines' (13:5, NIV) was fulfilled in a series of angry attacks, motivated in part by Samson's greatest weakness, an insatiable penchant for Philistine women;[13] the prophet Samuel (not otherwise known for his military prowess), Jonathan and Saul. For another, even the disastrous defeat at Aphek, which led to the deaths of 30,000 Israelite soldiers and the capture of the sacred ark of the covenant, had led to a surprisingly favourable turn of events—a lethal tour of the ark through Philistine territories, bringing plague and panic wherever it went (1 Samuel 4—6).

The Philistines seemed completely unimpressed by the Israelites and their leaders, yet they were consistently on edge when it came to Israel's God. This was a God who had brought the Israelites out of Egypt following a series of plagues and disasters.[14] This was a God whose presence inhabited the strange box that they'd captured in battle. This was a God who brought thunderstorms and hailstones and irrational fear and confusion wherever he went. It's not that the Philistines were unthinking in their acknowledgement of Israel's deity: in 1 Samuel 6:8–9 we see them conducting a scientific experiment to determine whether the epidemics across the Philistine cities were caused by the ark of the covenant or were just a coincidence. But the sight of the statue of Dagon lying headless and handless before the sacred box (5:1–4) was symbolic of the Philistines' deep-rooted unease in respect to the God of their enemies. Indeed, there are times in 1 Samuel when the Philistines could have taught the Israelites a thing or two about the 'fear of the Lord'.

Lesson three was that the leaders of the Israelites were generally victorious when they played to their God-given strengths. For Shamgar and Samson, that meant their physical prowess, which they combined with an ability to make the most of cattle prods and foxes' tails to cause mayhem among their opponents (Judges 3:31, 15:4–5). For Samuel it meant his gift of intercession, as he prayed his way to victory (1 Samuel 7:5–6). For Jonathan it meant using his head, as he recognised the psychological value of a small, local triumph on the way to achieving a larger national one (1 Samuel 14). In the virtual absence of conventional weaponry, a level of improvisation was called for, a creative inventiveness based on what each leader did best. The worst possible policy (as the defeat at Aphek demonstrated) was to try to match might with might, to enter some kind of unthinking arms race with their Philistine opponents.

And lesson four (the earliest of the lessons recorded in the Bible, but perhaps the hardest one for the Israelites to remember) was that the Philistines were there for two purposes, one practical and one spiritual. On a practical level, the book of Judges speaks of how the Philistines and their neighbours helped to 'teach warfare to the descendants of the Israelites who had not had previous battle experience' (3:2)—to keep them sharp, in other words. On a spiritual level, the same chapter informs us of the Philistines' role to 'test the Israelites to see whether they would obey the Lord's commands, which he had given their ancestors through Moses' (v. 4). The ongoing threat from Philistia kept Israel alert, revealing what was in her heart, reminding her of her dependence on God and acting as that 'thorn in the flesh' which Paul gradually learnt to value (2 Corinthians 12:7–9). A land flowing with milk and honey sounds a most enticing prospect, but a little roughage in the diet would enable Israel to keep fit and maintain her spiritual figure.

The significance of Azekah

As the Israelites and the Philistines gathered again for war, then, there was plenty of history between the two nations. On balance, perhaps, the Israelites were winning on points; yet few families can have remained unaffected by the devastating defeat at Aphek, with its tens of thousands of casualties among the fighting men of Israel.

The territory where this latest battle was to take place, though, had earlier, more positive memories for the

Israelite army: for the Philistines' latest incursion was near the lowland towns of Sokoh and Azekah, and Azekah had been the setting of a memorable victory (years before the Philistines became quite so troublesome) recorded for us in Joshua 10. The enemy on that occasion consisted of an alliance between five Amorite kings, including the king of Jerusalem, a name which makes its canonical debut in this chapter;[15] and Joshua's surprise attack on this powerful confederation was aided by massive hailstones and even, it was said, by the sun standing still. 'There has never been a day like it, before or since,' enthused the writer. 'Surely the Lord was fighting for Israel!' (v. 14).

Accordingly, as Saul and the Israelites faced the Philistines near Azekah, the very place of their encounter might have been expected to give them a psychological boost. A skilful leader would have ensured that the phrase from Joshua's day, 'Surely the Lord was fighting for Israel!' was resounding around the camp. It was a little like the English navy taking on new opponents off Cape Trafalgar, or the Scottish army fighting afresh at Bannockburn.

Centuries earlier, Joshua had been appointed by the Lord as Moses' successor, 'so that the Lord's people will not be like sheep without a shepherd' (Numbers 27:17). Under his leadership, this region had been wrested from the grip of those five Amorite kings and included within the inheritance of the tribe of Judah. And now Israel was looking for another shepherd to lead God's people and defeat this new confederation of five Philistine kings. What better setting than Azekah, where Joshua's memory remained fresh and inspirational, and where a hailstorm and the very length of the day had once been governed by the sovereign Yahweh, the all-powerful God of Israel?

Confidence and the call to reflection

Taking time out to reflect on Israel's history with her inveterate foes would have proved useful to Saul and his army; and there is something about the discipline of spiritual reflection—regularly reviewing our lives in the presence of a God who is both grace and truth—which is equally helpful, enabling us to learn from our victories and our defeats, and to grow in wisdom and godly confidence.

The Jesuits call this discipline the prayer of *examen*,[16] and helpfully teach a five-stage approach to such a practice.[17] First we recall that we are in the presence of God. Next we spend time reflecting on the blessings of the day. A period of silence follows, where we invite God's Spirit to help us look at our actions, attitudes and motives with honesty and patience. Then we review the day, responding to Paul's challenge to 'examine yourselves to see whether you are in the faith' (2 Corinthians 13:5). And finally we have a heart-to-heart talk with Jesus, where thanksgiving, confession and intercession combine to strengthen us and set us back on track.

It's just one approach to such a discipline. Others have so-called 'quiet times' to read the scriptures, reflect and pray, or include a period of reflection in their praying of the Daily Office, or keep a spiritual journal on a regular or occasional basis. But some commitment to personal reflection in the presence of God has always been a key component of Christian discipleship, and one which sorts out the spiritually mature from the also-rans.

There are many pressures and distractions, of course, which militate against the prayer of *examen* or its equivalents, and our natural tendency is to focus on the pressures of the present and the immediate future rather than to attend to the past or, indeed, to our long-term destiny. So we rush into each new situation with fresh anxiety, fresh confusion (or, indeed, fresh naivety) and without having properly banked the insight and godly confidence which our previous experiences should have developed within us. How many heresies, excesses and disappointments in the life of the church might have been prevented if only we'd known our church history a little better? It's an important and sobering question. And how much fear and muddle— how many foolish decisions and moral lapses—might have been avoided, had we built a greater discipline of personal reflection into our lives?

It's not simply individuals who should engage in a regular prayer of *examen*. Families, congregations, communities, even nations, may sometimes be called to a period of soul-searching, an honest review of the past conducted in the presence of a God who reveals, restores and forgives. We have already mentioned the Truth and Reconciliation Commission, a brave attempt to heal the wounds of South Africa's history by listening to the stories of oppressed and oppressor in the context of both grace and truth. We might also refer to the significant work of marriage counselling and family mediation, which seek to provide a similar kind of listening space on a personal level.

It takes a brave church leader to encourage his congregation to enter into the prayer of *examen* on behalf of the church, but many Christian communities would benefit from the experience. To bring the history of the church into the light—to acknowledge the good, the bad and the ugly that lies within the community of which we are a part—can be a deeply revealing experience as we seek to understand both the spiritual dynamics within the church and our relationship with those outside it. Such a process needs to be handled sensitively, but at best it enables the church to move onwards and upwards, rather than repeating the same old mistakes time and again.

In one of the churches with which I was connected, there was a history of broken marriages among its leadership, of abusive relationships within its membership and of total non-engagement with the community it was called upon to serve. On one occasion the practice of *examen* was followed by a service of confession, prayer, and a spiritual 'cleansing' of the church building and its surroundings; and how encouraging it is to see that a church from which the risen Christ had apparently removed the 'lampstand' of his presence (see Revelation 2:5) is now vibrant, healthy and drawing in new members almost every week.

So, what do we learn as we take the call to reflection seriously, whether as individuals or in families or church communities? And how can this call help us to grow in godly confidence? The lessons may be many and varied, but my hunch is that some, at least, will bear more than a passing resemblance to those gleaned from the history of the Israelites and Philistines in general and the story of David and Goliath in particular.

The Philistines were formidable opponents—and part of our growth in confidence relates to an ability to face up to the enemies outside and within, rather than giving way to a superficial optimism on the one hand or a debilitating pessimism on the other. This will be the theme of Chapter 2 as we join the Israelites in facing up to the sheer physicality of Goliath the Philistine giant.

The Philistines were not invincible—and equally essential to our confidence is the need to maintain the conviction that the living God is bigger than any problems we might face—that 'if God is for us, who can be against us?' (Romans 8:31). The varying responses of the Israelites to the Philistine threat (and David's call to a renewed faith in God's providence and power) will be examined in Chapters 3, 4 and 5.

The leaders of the Israelites were victorious when they played to their God-given strengths—and playing to *our* God-given strengths (as individuals and as a church) is another of the secrets of sure-footed Christian living, the godly self-confidence which provides the focus for Chapter 6 and a confidence in the gospel which we look at in Chapter 7.

And finally, *the Philistines were there for a purpose*—and the same can be true of the problems and challenges that assail us. Chapter 8 examines how it was the threatening presence of Goliath, together with the dazzling response of David, that transformed the situation; while Chapter 9 focuses on the aftermath of the battle, and the dangers of division once the external threat was passed.

So the Israelites and the Philistines face one another across the valley. The swords and javelins are sharpened on one side, the mattocks and axes on the other. The worlds of *The Iliad* and of the Bible prepare to collide. Let battle commence!

— 2 —

Confidence, Faith and Wishful Thinking: Introducing Goliath

In his bestseller *Good to Great*, management guru Jim Collins tells of a meeting he held with Admiral Jim Stockdale, where the two men discussed the Admiral's imprisonment in a Vietnamese prisoner-of-war camp. Stockdale was showered with 26 personal combat decorations on his release in recognition of the extraordinary courage that he demonstrated over eight years of incarceration. 'How on earth did you do it?' was the question Collins put to him as they walked side by side, Stockdale limping on his stiff leg that was the result of repeated torture.

'I never lost faith in the end of the story,' was Stockdale's response: 'I never doubted not only that I would get out, but also that I would prevail in the end and turn the experience into the defining event of my life.'

As the walk continued, another question occurred to Collins: 'Who didn't make it out?' he asked. 'Oh, that's easy,' replied Stockdale. 'The optimists. They were the ones who said, "We're going to be out by Christmas." And Christmas would come, and Christmas would go. Then they'd say, "We're going to be out by Easter." And Easter would come, and Easter would go. And then Thanksgiving, and then it would be Christmas again. And they died of a broken heart.'

'This is a very important lesson,' concluded Stockdale: 'You must never confuse faith that you will prevail in the end—which you cannot afford to lose—with the discipline to confront the most brutal facts of your current reality, whatever they might be.'[1]

Although the author of 1 Samuel 17 was not acquainted with the 'Stockdale Paradox' (as Collins went on to describe it), there's no question of his commitment to 'confront the most brutal facts of your current reality, whatever they might be'. The description of Goliath of Gath is a masterly example of good storytelling which brilliantly conveys the sheer power and presence of Israel's mighty opponent; and the cumulative effect of his height, his armour and his relentless howls of derision make him a kind of archetype for all bullies everywhere.

The Incredible Hulk

A champion named Goliath, who was from Gath, came out of the Philistine camp. His height was six cubits and a span. He had a bronze helmet on his head and wore a coat of scale armour of bronze weighing five thousand shekels; on his legs he wore bronze greaves, and a bronze javelin was slung on his back. His spear shaft was like a weaver's rod, and its iron point weighed six hundred shekels. His shield-bearer went ahead of him.

Goliath stood and shouted to the ranks of Israel, 'Why do you come out and line up for battle? Am I not a Philistine, and are you not the servants of Saul? Choose a man and let him come down to me. If he is able to fight and kill me, we will become your subjects; but if I overcome him and kill him, you will become our subjects and serve us.' Then the Philistine said, 'This day I defy the armies of Israel! Give me a man and let us fight each other.'

1 SAMUEL 17:4–10

Who was this Goliath? His name may have its roots in Anatolia (in modern-day Turkey[2]), which would suggest that his forebears were among the Aegean 'Sea Peoples' who colonised the land of Canaan more than two centuries earlier. He has the distinction of being the first named Philistine in the Bible, which up till this point always speaks of Philistines in the plural, but never of a Philistine in the singular; and his title of 'champion' means literally 'one who fights between the battle lines'—in other words, a man who steps out from the front of his army to throw down the gauntlet to the opposing side.[3]

Was Goliath a giant? Certainly one of the oldest of the texts available to us describes him as 'six cubits and a span', which would place him above the nine-foot mark, and several inches above the tallest of men.[4] The Septuagint and the Samuel scrolls discovered at Qumran,[5] on the other hand, reduce him to a mere four cubits (perhaps six foot nine), a height which would still have been formidable enough by the standards of the day. In Goliath, it seems, we are not looking at a giant in the 'Jack and the Beanstalk' sense, but we are still faced with a man of considerable bulk and stature: a highly intimidating sight as he stood there, his armour gleaming in the sun.

It's to that armour that the narrator next turns, as he talks us through the bronze helmet, the coat of armour, the greaves (which protected the legs), the javelin[6] and the spear, before mentioning the shield-bearer who 'went ahead of him' as a first line of defence and (presumably) a kind of caddy. A further weapon, Goliath's mighty sword, is not mentioned at this point, although it features later in the story (vv. 45, 51) and may well have been in the caddy's bag. While we're told about the impressive weight of the suit of armour (59kg) and of the iron point[7] of the spear (7kg), all we hear of the sword is that 'there is none like it' (21:9)—the phrase again implying a highly impressive piece of military hardware. And the reference to the spear as like a 'weaver's rod' is also suggestive, with rope wrapped round the weapon to give it additional weight and force.

The only part of Goliath's body which remained unprotected was his face. Both armour and weaponry were highly impressive—but nowhere in the description do we read of a visor.

It is possible to see parallels between this passage and several episodes in Homer's *The Iliad*. In Book 3, for example, we find Paris putting on his armour before a one-on-one combat between himself and Menelaus.

[Paris] began by tying around his legs a pair of splendid greaves, which were fitted with sliver clips for the ankles. Next he put on a cuirass [plated armour] on his breast... Over his shoulder he slung a bronze sword with a silver-studded hilt, and then a great thick shield. On his sturdy head he set a well-made helmet... Lastly he took up a powerful spear, which was fitted to his grip.[8]

Homer often seems more captivated with the *style* of the armour than does his biblical counterpart: both Agamemnon's armour and Achilles' shield are lovingly described as things of great beauty,[9] while Goliath's armour is impressive but functional. Yet the links are still there, which is perhaps unsurprising given Goliath's probable Aegean ancestry.

The height, the armour, and then there's the voice! Goliath's challenge to the Israelite army was loud and intimidating, with the perfect balance between derision and aggression. Comparing himself to his opponents, Goliath stated that he was a 'Philistine' (literally, '*The* Philistine', implying freedom, courage, independence, pride) while they were merely the slaves of Saul (and look at him, the wimp, skulking there in the shadows!). 'Choose a man' was the challenge (since clearly Saul didn't match that description), 'and have him come down to me'.

This form of taunting abuse was also practised by the protagonists in *The Iliad*, and there's no question that Goliath was horribly good at it. It's true that he may have shared his compatriots' reluctance to challenge Israel's God (choosing instead the softer target of the ranks of Israel), but everything else about Goliath spoke of a complete self-belief, a kind of arrogant swagger which was extremely hard to counter. The Israelites were completely paralysed by the sight and sound of this man; and meanwhile the Philistine army were no doubt delighted to have found a champion of such style and bravado, especially given the alarming nature of some of their previous encounters with Israel and her God.

It's a sign of Goliath's complete mastery of the situation that no one thought to question whether or not he was entitled to dictate the terms on which the battle should be fought. It was simply the bully who set the rules (as is so often the case, from the smallest of personal vendettas to the most widespread of conflicts and trade disputes). They were unusual rules, for Israel at least; for while the duel was a familiar concept in Greek culture (with 28 examples in *The Iliad* alone) the Hebrews had never before settled a contest in this way.[10] Perhaps the ethos of 'the champion' had begun to percolate into Hebrew culture from the moment the Israelites asked for a king 'to lead us and to go out before us and fight our battles' (1 Samuel 8:20). But the idea that Goliath alone should dictate the ground on which they should fight, the rules by which they should fight and the manner by which the fight should be settled was patently unjust—and even more so when his opponent would have the disadvantage of coming down to Goliath, rather than Goliath going up to him.

The duel is, in theory, a relatively bloodless way to settle the score. When Paris and Menelaus proposed a duel over Helen in Book 3 of *The Iliad* we're told that the Trojans were 'delighted at the prospect of a reprieve from the painful business of fighting'.[11] In reality, though, many of *The Iliad*'s duels ended up with an uncertain outcome, and even those that were conclusive didn't generally carry much weight. As Goliath threw down the gauntlet in these verses, too, promising that if he was defeated the Philistines would become the subjects of the Israelites, there may well have been a healthy dose of scepticism around. The battle between Goliath and his opponent would have massive psychological implications for both the winning and the losing side, but whether the losers would simply lie down and accept the terms of the contest was a decidedly moot point.

And just one final observation to complete this portrait of the Philistine champion: the Hebrew word for 'defy' in verse 10 will play a central role in the rest of this chapter, and indeed in many of Israel's later skirmishes with her Philistine neighbours. In these verses Goliath believed that he was 'defying' the ranks of Israel, a rather motley band of men who were poorly led and equally poorly armed: an easy target for someone of such swagger and confidence. But every now and then it transpires that the victim of a bully has a friend (or perhaps a father) who is strong, intimidating and enraged. And despite his fighting talk, perhaps Goliath's memory of the plague and panic which had accompanied the presence of the ark of the covenant in his home town of Gath should have given him more than a little pause for thought.

Confronting the brutal facts today

As we pictured Saul and his men gathered around the campfire in the valley of Elah in the last chapter, the first lesson that we identified was that the Philistines were indeed formidable opponents. In Goliath that lesson was now focused on one man—The Philistine rather than the Philistines. And there is something about the discipline to 'confront the most brutal facts of your current reality, whatever they might be' (the Stockdale Paradox) that remains foundational to genuine confidence, freeing us from the debilitating effects of wishful thinking and frequent disappointment, and enabling us to square up to life as it is.

There are various English words and phrases which describe the opposite tendency—escapism, avoidance, denial, 'having your head in the sand', 'ignoring the elephant in the room'—and each implies a kind of moral cowardice, however understandable the desire to pretend or escape can sometimes be. Two images from Britain's past illustrate the point with clarity: one the picture of Neville Chamberlain in September 1938, brandishing his non-aggression pact with Hitler while proclaiming 'Peace for our time'; the other the sight of Winston Churchill addressing the British Parliament just 20 months later and stating bluntly, 'I have nothing to offer but blood, toil, tears and sweat.' It is easy to have sympathy for Chamberlain in his longing for peace, yet there is no question that Churchill's approach was far more realistic and motivating. 'There is no worse mistake in public leadership', as he later put it, 'than to hold out false hopes soon to be swept away.'[12]

What, then, are the brutal facts that confront us today?

For many around the world, Goliath takes the form of a vicious and repressive regime, which seeks to manipulate and bully its citizens into submission. On a visit to East Germany in the early 1980s, the full extent of the state's power over its people was graphically expressed in the gun-toting *Stasi* (the secret police force) and in the ubiquitous presence of large red banners proclaiming the glories of the Socialist Unity Party. A teenager I met, called Magdalena, had courageously refused to participate in the *Jugendweihe*, a kind of communist confirmation service at which young people pledged their allegiance to the party and its humanist ideals. As a result—and because Goliath had set the rules—she was barred from attending university, and was reduced to working as an orderly in a hospital where she should have been a surgeon.

For others, Goliath is a distorted idea or prejudice, perhaps even a cultural ideal which is harsh or unattainable. During their 16 years as medical missionaries in China, there were various such 'ideals' which my grandparents felt the need to challenge, among them the prevalence of bound feet. The process, which would begin at the age of four or five, included the deliberate breaking of four of the toes on each foot, and the tight binding of the foot in bandages, resulting in agonising pain and debilitating infection. Although the practice was being seriously questioned by the time my grandparents arrived in the early 1920s, my grandmother still recalled the 'women hobbling about on their misshapen bound feet' and wrote of how it was 'unthinkable that a girl child should not undergo this torture: only working women had big feet!'[13]

The voices of the so-called 'new atheism' have been harsh and aggressive in recent years, and bestsellers such as Richard Dawkins *The God Delusion* (Bantam, 2006) or Christopher Hitchens' *God Is Not Great* (Atlantic, 2007) make Goliath himself seem positively deferential in his attitude towards the 'ranks of Israel' and their God. There are times in her past when the church has behaved considerably more like Goliath than David, and these are picked on with glee by the new atheists, as they scan the course of world history through a peculiarly selective pair of cultural glasses. But it's not just the church (or its equivalent in other religious traditions) which comes under attack. Dawkins is deliberately provocative in his descriptions of the God of the Old Testament, calling him variously 'a petty, unjust, unforgiving control freak', a 'vindictive, bloodthirsty ethnic cleanser', and 'arguably the most unpleasant character in all fiction'.[14]

Alongside these more extravagant attacks, thoughtful Christians note, too, a quieter shift in values, perceptions and social norms affecting the practice of their faith. The narrative of church decline is regularly trumpeted by the media, a story all too often supported by the experience of gently ageing congregations and finances that don't quite stretch like they used to. A church used to setting the rules—to the security of Christendom—now finds itself on the backfoot in a way reminiscent of that small retreating triangular flag in the opening credits of *Dad's Army*. It's no wonder that Christian confidence can be in short supply.

What of our personal Goliaths? They may appear in many shapes and forms, although they are not perhaps as unique as we sometimes fear them to be: 'no temptation has overtaken you,' writes Paul, 'except what is common to us all' (1 Corinthians 10:13). In his later correspondence with the Corinthians, Paul could speak of 'great pressure, far beyond our ability to endure', of 'conflicts on the outside, fears within', and of his famous 'thorn in the flesh', which may have been a disability, an illness or an especially trying individual (see 2 Corinthians 1:8; 7:5; 12:7–8). In our own experience, too, particular fears, temptations, difficulties, discouragements, self-doubts, accusations or addictions may seem as intractable and menacing as the mighty Philistine himself, and shout at us with just the same tone of ridicule in their voices. In one recent pastoral encounter the 'Goliath' was a father whose perceived criticism was continuing to cause great damage to his son's career path, relationships and self-esteem long after the father himself had died.

It's easy to personalise the opposition; but ultimately the battles we face go far beyond individuals and are part of a bigger picture than we're generally aware of. This picture incorporates both the work of God within us (keeping us spiritually on the ball, as the Philistines were mandated to do for the Israelites in Judges 3) and the spiritual warfare which invariably accompanies the spread of God's kingdom. In his letter to the Ephesians, Paul was writing from the context of a prison cell, which he inhabited courtesy of the Roman authorities. Even within that setting, with his enemy apparently sitting there in the form of a heavily armed Roman guard, Paul could recognise that 'our struggle is not against flesh and blood, but against the rulers, against the authorities, against the powers of this dark world and against the spiritual forces of evil in the heavenly realms' (Ephesians 6tr6:12).

A philosophical diversion

There's a further possible 'take' on this passage which regards the formidable bulk of Goliath in a rather more philosophical light, for if this Philistine is seen as an early representative of the world of the ancient Greeks, there's something about his challenge which is strangely familiar in our continuing struggles between the forces of faith and the new atheism—a struggle in which *The God Delusion* and *God Is Not Great* are just recent manifestations. In his short book *Proper Confidence: Faith, doubt and certainty in Christian discipleship* (SPCK, 1995) Lesslie Newbigin reminds us that the uniqueness of European culture is founded on the fact that, for a thousand years, 'the barbarian tribes who had found their home there were schooled in both the biblical story and the learning of classical antiquity, the legacy of Greece and Rome' (p. 3). From the beginning of Europe's history as a distinct entity, there has been an ongoing tension between Greek rationality and the world of the Bible.

Rationality and revelation will always make strange bedfellows, and it's hardly surprising that some have concluded that the bed isn't big enough for the two of them. 'What has Jerusalem in common with Athens?' asked Tertullian in the early third century, assuming the answer 'Nothing'. Others have accepted Goliath's challenge to 'come down to me', and have sought to fight the battle (or more often to conduct a vigorous debate) on some kind of common ground. Origen of Alexandria, a contemporary of Tertullian, did just that, while a thousand years later another great academic, Thomas Aquinas, took the approach further, achieving, in Newbigin's words, 'a synthesis of the new learning with the old biblical tradition, a synthesis which was to shape the thinking of Western Christendom to this day'.[15]

We will be returning to Newbigin's argument in Chapter 10, but while Goliath seems to have demonstrated nothing of the finesse or philosophical brilliance of the intellectual 'giants' of ancient Greece, there is something of his confidence in *himself* which contrasts sharply with the Yahweh-focused faith of Abraham, Moses and Samuel. It's not that the best of the classical world necessarily shared Goliath's chutzpah, let alone his arrogant reliance on sheer brute power. But a biblical critique of this philosophy would warn us of the dangers of relying too heavily on our own advantages and abilities, whether brain or brawn, our status or our pedigree. 'If others think they have reasons to put confidence in the flesh, I have more,' writes Paul, speaking of his faultless lineage and impressive CV: 'but whatever were gains for me I now consider loss for the sake of Christ' (Philippians 3:4, 7). 'His pleasure is not in the strength of the horse, nor his delight in the power of human legs,' writes the psalmist, referring to a rather more Goliath-like brand of self-reliance; 'the Lord delights in those who fear him, who put their hope in his unfailing love' (Psalm 147:10–11).

Goliath had plenty of flesh (and highly toned flesh at that!) in which to place his confidence. He also gloried in his state-of-the-art armour and weaponry, and, we might surmise, had employed the best shield-bearing caddy that money could buy. And while this book will later argue for a right kind of self-confidence (one based on a humble recognition of the abilities which God has given to us), Goliath's confidence was not of that sort. Had he had time to write an autobiography, I suspect he might have beaten Muhammad Ali to the title *Greatest: My Own Story*.[16]

The attractions of denial

Neville Chamberlain's famous promise of 'Peace for our time' is one of thousands of examples throughout history which point to both the attractions and the dangers of wishful thinking. In the Old Testament we are introduced to various false prophets—the men of Jeremiah's day, for example— who exhibited this tendency to an alarming degree. 'They dress the wound of my people as though it were not serious,' complained the Lord through Jeremiah. '"Peace, peace," they say, when there is no peace' (6:14). In the New Testament, we witness Peter fluctuating between the roles of true and false prophet. At one moment he was proclaiming, 'You are the Christ, the Son of the living God', earning for himself praise because he had truly heard from the 'Father in heaven' (Matthew 16:16–17, NIV). At the next—perhaps buoyed by his success the first time round—he was reproving his master as Jesus began to spell out the tough nature of that calling: 'Never, Lord!' he said. 'This shall never happen to you!', earning for himself the toughest of reprimands: 'Get behind me, Satan' (16:22–23).

An Inconvenient Truth[17] is the title of a well-known environmental tract by former presidential hopeful Al Gore, focusing on one of the biggest Goliaths of them all, global warming. Some of the particular claims in the documentary have since been disputed, but it's increasingly hard to argue with Gore's overall conclusions, or with the logic of the film's title. For truth, all too often, is either inconvenient or something worse. For Jeremiah it meant acknowledging the power of the Babylonian Goliath who would shortly sweep in and enslave the people of Jerusalem and Judea. For Peter it meant admitting that Jesus knew rather better than he did what the calling of the Messiah was truly to be, a calling both to suffer and to die. For humankind it means embracing a change of lifestyle, probably of a radical nature, to help bring us back into harmony with the rest of God's creation.

Wishful thinking is a major problem within the church, too, for the sheer power of the forces of secularism and indifference has all too often been ignored at both a national and a grassroots level up until the point (at least) when the money runs out. The church in England is here indebted to the work of statistician Peter Brierley, who has charted the numerical progress of the church (in general, a downward progress) over the past 20 years or more; and the very titles of Brierley's books demonstrate both the strength of this particular Goliath and the author's unease, sometimes exasperation, at the church's tendency to stick her head in the sand in response: *Act on the Facts* (1992); *Twelve Things to Wake Up To* (1999); *The Tide Is Running Out* (2000); *Pulling Out of the Nosedive* (2006).[18] Of course there are plenty of good stories to tell as well, and fellow statistician Bob Jackson tells them with particular insight and enthusiasm.[19] But there's little question that the words of Admiral Stockdale should find a place on every church leader's desk, from the humblest of deacons to the most reverent of archbishops: 'You must never confuse faith that you will prevail in the end—which you cannot afford to lose—with the discipline to confront the most brutal facts of your current reality, whatever they might be.'

On a personal level, denial often seems an easier option than acknowledging 'the most brutal facts of our current reality', though the long-term effect of such an approach can be devastating. One of the greatest frustrations for those involved in marriage and relationship counselling lies in the fact that most couples arrive at that point far too late, when the Goliaths in their relationship have really got a hold. One of the greatest sadnesses in pastoral ministry is the sight of a person failing to admit the pressures around them and within them until everything dramatically collapses in the devastation of a nervous breakdown, a serious midlife crisis or even suicide. Even the Christian healing ministry—a wonderful reflection of the compassion and power of Christ—can all too easily be misused by those who have bought into this culture of denial; and I may not be the only pastor who has been virtually excluded from the bedside of a terminally sick patient by an apparently 'faith-filled' relative, because of my belief that there are times to prepare people for their death and not to continue praying for their physical healing and restoration.

Some Christians are caricatured as being paranoid about the 'wiles of the devil', too ready to find a demon under every bed, and on occasions the criticism can be justified. But a far more common tendency among most Christians is a complete disregard for the spiritual powers behind the struggles we face and thus, on occasions, a serious misjudgement of our own abilities both to cope with them and to take them on. Peter's instruction to the church of his day, 'Be self-controlled and alert. Your enemy the devil prowls around like a roaring lion looking for someone to devour' (1 Peter 5:8, NIV) may sound a little melodramatic to some. But a greater alertness to the 'spiritual forces of evil in the heavenly realms' (Ephesians 6:12) would, I suspect, make us far more effective as soldiers of Christ, rather than keeping us at a level of minimal impact on the world around us.

Even in the philosophical realm it is easy to underestimate our opponents. The Goliath of atheism, for example, which cut such a fine figure across many parts of the world from the French Revolution onwards, is no longer the force it once was, a trend that is brilliantly charted by Alister McGrath in his book *The Twilight of Atheism: The Rise and Fall of Disbelief in the Modern World* (Rider, 2004). Yet the very popularity of the works of Dawkins and Hitchens—the fact that they have remained in the bestselling charts for months on end— suggests that it's a little too early to write the obituary for this particular philosophical movement. Could it be that there's a large Philistine army out there who are entirely unimpressed by the church as they perceive it, but who retain the vestiges of a sense of the 'fear of the Lord'? Could it be, too, that this army is both cheered and relieved when a champion steps forward on their behalf to say things they would never dare to say themselves, and so relieve them of the need to be polite (let alone deferential) to the Christian God?

In future chapters we will focus on the first part of the Stockdale Paradox—the 'faith that you will prevail in the end', which places hope right at the heart of the Christian endeavour. But ours is not to be an easy optimism characterised by superficiality, blandness, avoidance or denial; and nor is it to be a confidence in the flesh, a sense that our own strength, energy and cleverness will somehow see us through. Instead the author of 1 Samuel 17 gives us a highly impressive picture of the archetypal bully, and encourages us to face him head on: for this is the surprising gateway to a genuinely *Christian* confidence, a confidence based on reality and not on wishful thinking. It's an extension of the discipline of our last chapter, the Jesuit practice of *examen*, but this time we are not reflecting on the past, and learning from its lessons. This time we are grappling with the present, a present which is up, close and personal, and which calls for a clear and decisive response.

— 3 —

Confidence within God's Church: Introducing Saul and the Israelites

When driving through the countryside on a dark night it is not unusual to come across a rabbit crouching in the middle of the road. The rabbit has the strength and turn of speed to respond quite easily to the challenge, and hop away out of danger, but instead it sits there, seemingly mesmerised by the headlights of the approaching vehicle, and unable to move. It is the worst kind of fear imaginable, a response which simply invites disaster; and only with the greatest skill and presence of mind is it possible for the driver to spot the rabbit in time and avoid a collision.

To compare today's church to that rabbit might seem unfair. But in many parts of the church (especially in the West) there is a kind of defeatism around, a disastrous loss of nerve which leads to paralysis in the face of the secular juggernaut. On a corporate level, that tendency finds expression in the defensive position that the church all too often seems to be occupying, desperately fighting (like many a former colonial power) to retain some small fraction of her past influence or busying herself with ever more defensive bureaucracy. On an individual level, it is lived out in the actions of a million Christian believers who've learnt that the best way to stay out of trouble at work or at school is to keep your head down and shut up about your Christian convictions.

The reason for this unhappy situation is not hard to find. Since the days of the Enlightenment the church has come under sustained attack as foolish and ridiculous on the one hand, divisive and dangerous on the other. On a recent holiday I much enjoyed rereading *The Moonstone* by Wilkie Collins, one of the earliest and greatest detective novels (published 1868).[1] Collins' picture of Drusilla Clack (a formidable character who looks for every opportunity to scatter religious tracts around the house of her aunt, Lady Verinder) is a brilliant send-up, forcibly reminding us of the woman of C.S. Lewis' acquaintance who 'lived for others; and you could tell the others by the hunted look on their faces'. And it would take a peculiarly touchy individual to be seriously offended by Wilkie Collins' brand of satirical humour, but the cumulative effect of a thousand and one Miss Clacks and worse in numerous novels, plays, soaps and movies can be seriously discouraging, even debilitating, for the Christian disciple.

There is, though, a deeper root to the frequent lack of confidence among today's believers, and that is to be found in the church's tendency from its earliest days to place far too much responsibility on the shoulders of a small number of (generally paid) professionals and far too little responsibility on the shoulders of everyone else. Solving this conundrum—releasing the massive potential of the whole people of God—is arguably the church's greatest challenge today. Some have even argued the need for a new reformation, a rediscovery of the 'priesthood of all believers', a renewed sense that we are the body of Christ, the army of God, and more than conquerors through Christ who loves us (see Romans 8:37).

Trapped in the headlights

On hearing the Philistine's words, Saul and all the Israelites were dismayed and terrified.

1 SAMUEL 17:11

As we move from Goliath and the ranks of Philistia, and focus on Saul and his army, that picture of a mesmerised rabbit—indeed a whole bunch of mesmerised rabbits—is peculiarly apt. The 'oncoming vehicle' in this case was both powerful and formidable, and it is hardly surprising that those 'rabbits' were dazzled by the sheer bulk of that vehicle, by the swagger and overweening confidence with which it was driven, by the blast of its horn and the sparkling brilliance of its bodywork. Bullies always have a paralysing effect on their victims, and Goliath, as we have seen, was the archetypal bully.[2]

Yet there's more to this picture than meets the eye. These 'rabbits' were not as powerless as they seemed. We have been reminded in Chapter 2 of how Shamgar, Samson, Samuel, Jonathan and Saul himself had defeated the Philistines on previous occasions; of how the ark of the covenant had caused havoc in their midst; of how even Gath, Goliath's home town, had been afflicted by tumours and a communal panic attack, presumably at just the time when Goliath was at his youngest and most impressionable (1 Samuel 5:8–9). And the question is therefore this: what is it about the 'rabbits' which kept them crouching in the middle of the road, rather than taking evasive or even aggressive action (for these were potential Super Rabbits!)? Why, 'on hearing the Philistine's words', did Saul and all the Israelites end up quite so 'dismayed and terrified'?

The answer is found in one of the most significant chapters of the Old Testament, 1 Samuel 8, where the Israelites pressed Samuel to find them a king. For many years, Israel had experimented with different models of leadership: Moses the pioneer; Joshua the military general; Deborah and Samson, the so-called judges; Samuel the prophet. But even a successful leader like Gideon was in no doubt that his role was essentially a secondary one. As he put it towards the end of his life, 'I will not rule over you, nor will my son rule over you. The Lord will rule over you' (Judges 8:23). There was an undoubted need for human under-shepherds—no one ever denied that—but as Gideon's speech makes clear, Israel's primary call was to follow the one true Shepherd, to remain at heart a theocratic society.

Yet when the elders of Israel called on their leader in 1 Samuel 8, all was about to change. 'You are old,' they said to Samuel, 'and your sons do not walk in your ways; now appoint a king to lead us, such as all the other nations have' (v. 5). It may not have been the most diplomatic or tactful of speeches, but its logic was impeccable. Samuel *was* old, well past any normal retirement age. His sons *were* a liability, and tales of their dishonesty and acceptance of bribes were widespread. Samuel himself was still respected as a man of considerable personal integrity with a virtual hotline to the Almighty, but the question of his successor had become a pressing one, and the obvious solution was staring them in the face. Every other nation had a king, and now the elders wanted a king too.

The motivation of those elders may well have been sincere—but alongside any personal hurt and sense of rejection, their request sent shivers down Samuel's spine; and as he prayed, it became clear that God himself shared in the prophet's unease. In calling for a human king, the elders seemed to be turning away from their heavenly king, from their unique calling to model what it meant to be God's holy people. In the words of Walter Brueggemann, kingship was 'an old and well-established phenomenon in Israel's international context', but was 'new, problematic and dangerous for Israel... Early Israel had emerged precisely as a subversive alternative to human kingship.'[3]

Samuel, however, was called to listen to the elders—indeed to grant their request—but only after he'd issued a stern health warning to the Israelites, spelling out the oppressive nature of what they were asking for (vv. 11–18). It was an excellent speech, especially when delivered to a people whose history included centuries of oppression under a succession of Egyptian Pharaohs: as health warnings go, it could hardly have been spelt out more clearly. But as many a Health Minister has discovered, health warnings, however garish, are often astonishingly ineffective. The people refused to listen to Samuel. 'No!' they said. 'We want a king over us'; and then that ominous sentence: 'Then we shall be like all the other nations, with a king to lead us and to go out before us and fight our battles' (vv. 19–20).

Two phrases in that response are of great relevance as we study the 'rabbits' mesmerised in the dazzling headlights of Goliath the Philistine. 'Then we shall be like all the other nations' speaks of the Israelites' desire to emulate the pagan forms of leadership that they saw among the Philistines, Midianites and Moabites around them; while the request for a 'king to lead us and to go out before us and fight our battles' suggests the fullest possible delegation of responsibility from a people to a single representative individual. Both sentiments, as we will see, would have disastrous consequences; and both continue to affect (and infect) the witness of God's people today.

In 1 Samuel 17, then, we find the Israelites 'dismayed and terrified' by the challenge of Goliath, and looking to a king whose job description included the call to 'lead us and go out before us and fight our battles'. But in the event the only pre-eminence that Saul held as Israel's leader was a primacy of place among the mesmerised: 'On hearing the Philistine's words, *Saul* and all the Israelites were dismayed and terrified.' What was it about King Saul that had so robbed him of his confidence? How is it that this man, chosen by God, anointed by Samuel, endorsed by the ranks of Israel—a leader with some considerable military achievements already under his belt—should have ended up quite so paralysed in the face of the Goliath juggernaut?

Saul: a cautionary tale

The portrayal of Saul, son of Kish, in the first book of Samuel is one of the most brilliant psychological studies in ancient literature. Saul is first introduced to us as 'an impressive young man without equal among the Israelites—a head taller than any of the others' (9:2, NIV), but this striking introduction is tempered by the mundane task he is set by his father: an expedition to chase a bunch of recalcitrant donkeys who have made a bid for freedom across the hills of central Israel. As with young David, who later met his destiny while delivering cheeses to his brothers on the battlefield (17:18), Saul's humdrum expedition took a dramatic turn as he found himself face-to-face with Samuel. The prophet duly put his mind at rest about the donkeys, cooked a slap-up meal for his bewildered guest, provided him with a bed for the night, and finally anointed him as Israel's future leader (neither Samuel nor the Almighty could quite bring themselves to use the 'k' word at this point).[4] Saul was then empowered by the Spirit of the Lord and welcomed by the people—the first time they had ever had cause to shout 'Long live the king!' (10:24)—and his appointment was enthusiastically confirmed following a victory over a particularly sadistic foe, Nahash the Ammonite, who had threatened to gouge out the right eye of all the inhabitants of one of the local towns (11:1–11).

Even at this early stage, though, there are signs that all was not well with Saul. For one thing, his very appointment was made despite some deep unease on the part of God, Samuel and a vocal minority among the people of Israel.[5] For another, that concern seemed to be shared by Saul himself. Before his private anointing, he described himself to Samuel as 'a Benjamite, from the smallest tribe of Israel', then continued, 'and is not my clan the least of all the clans of the tribe of Benjamin?' (9:21). Before his public anointing this same diffidence was expressed by his decision to hide among the baggage in a desperate last-ditch attempt to avoid the call of God (10:22).

Diffidence, of course, can be an attractive quality. There is a long and honourable tradition in church history (and indeed in the scriptures themselves) of men and women responding to God's call with a sense of their own unworthiness and inadequacy. But in Saul's case the insecurity was far more worrying. Here was a man given to fits of depression, an inner turmoil which could only be relieved by the balm of beautiful music (16:14–16). Here was a man who would later become consumed with jealousy, quite unjustly portraying David as a traitor and rabble-rouser. Here was a man whose reaction to an admittedly tactless popular song—'Saul has slain his thousands, and David his tens of thousands'[6]—

would lead him into a long and increasingly frantic chase across the Judean desert in a desperate attempt to catch up with David and take his life. Indeed, 'catching up with David' would become both Saul's obsession and his downfall.

It's quite possible to regard Saul in the role of tragic hero, a biblical prototype for Shakespeare's Othello, the Moor of Venice, whose insecurity and jealousy would lead him down a similarly irrational and murderous path. Saul, it could be argued, was given an impossible task in the most ambiguous of circumstances, anointed by both Samuel and God for a role in which neither Samuel nor God (nor, quite possibly, Saul himself) believed. Perhaps, we might argue, hiding among the baggage was the most rational thing he ever did, especially given his known propensity for insecurity and depression.

Yet to see Saul purely as a victim of his circumstances is to misread 1 Samuel. For by the time he was confronted by Goliath in chapter 17, Saul was compromised as a leader, and not simply insecure in the role assigned to him. We might feel that Saul was placed in an impossible position by Samuel in chapter 13, when the prophet was late for an appointment and Saul foolishly responded by offering sacrifices himself on the eve of a battle. But the incident two chapters later was far less pardonable, where Saul clearly disobeyed the Lord's instructions in the full flush of his victory over the Amalekites,[7] then compounded his crime through the most impressive series of evasive answers since the garden of Eden.

The circumstances may differ, but Saul's roasting at the hands of Samuel (see 15:12–31) is all too familiar to viewers of today's news programmes, with Samuel acting as the toughest of interrogators. The course of Saul's answers is also familiar, and has been broadly emulated by a steady trickle of politicians faced with the charge of corruption or ineptitude. First, 'I didn't do it'; then, 'My men did it, but they had the best possible motives'; then again, 'Well, yes, their motives weren't perfect, but part of what they were planning to do was good and proper'; and finally, 'OK, OK. I did it as well. Now are you satisfied? I was frightened of the men, so I got swept along with it all. I'm sorry—and now let's forget about it and go and worship together' (or, more probably in today's climate, 'Let's go and have a drink!').

There's one particular phrase which first escapes Saul's lips during the course of the interview, and which is both sad and telling. Faced with the wrath of Samuel, Saul referred to Yahweh as 'the Lord *your* God' (15:15); and from then on the die was cast, as the Spirit of the Lord departed from Saul, to be replaced by the 'evil spirit' of his doubts and insecurity (16:14).[8]

Confidence and the people of God

The people's request for a king in 1 Samuel 8 has some powerful parallels in the history of the church: for from the second century AD onwards the radical vision of the church as a 'chosen people, a royal priesthood, a holy nation, a people belonging to God' (1 Peter 2:9, NIV) has been subverted time and again by individualistic, even 'heroic', models of leadership—models which in their turn have created a kind of caste system, with clergy, missionaries, monks and nuns at the top and (in some circles, at least) bankers, lawyers and stockbrokers somewhere near the bottom! As R. Paul Stevens puts it, 'Throughout almost all its history the church has been composed of two categories of people: those who "do" ministry and those to whom it is "done".'[9]

This state of affairs is far removed from anything we see in the New Testament—for while the great Reformation phrase 'the priesthood of all believers' is itself based on fairly narrow biblical foundations,[10] the overall balance of the New Testament is clearly weighted in favour of the people of God—a people called, gifted, empowered, commissioned—rather than perpetuating some specious clergy/laity divide. R. Paul Stevens helpfully points out that there is no such thing as 'laity' in the New Testament, and further that all Christians are described as 'clergy'. While the word *laos* (people) appears on several occasions, the more disparaging *laikos* (layman) is entirely absent. *Kleros*, on the other hand—from which we derive the word 'clergy'—is present in a number of places, and means literally a part or share or inheritance. 'I am sending you to [the Gentiles],' said the risen Christ to Paul, 'to open their eyes and turn them from darkness to light… so that they may receive forgiveness of sins and a place [*kleron*] among those who are sanctified by faith in me' (Acts 26:17–18).[11]

It is true that there are leaders in the New Testament, who generally work together as a team—apostles, overseers, elders and deacons—but there is not the slightest suggestion that these should form some kind of professional élite, or that the words 'royal' or 'priesthood' should be applied to them in any exclusive way. Jesus alerted his disciples to the dangers of just this tendency in a passage reminiscent of Samuel's health warning in 1 Samuel 8: 'You know that the rulers of the Gentiles lord it over them, and their high officials exercise authority over them. Not so with you…' (Matthew 20:25–26).[12] The whole ethos of the Church from the day of Pentecost onwards was rather founded on the burning conviction that the Lord had at last fulfilled Joel's ancient prophecy and had 'poured out his Spirit on all people' (see Joel 2:28; Acts 2:17).

It wasn't long, however, before the same motivation which drove the Israelite elders to ask Samuel for a king found expression in the life of the early Church, primarily as a response to the threat not of Philistines but of heretics. In the Greek city-state, the people (*laos*) were distinguished from their leaders (*kleroi*), and the early Christians' desire to 'be like all the other nations' suggested that a similar approach should be adopted within the Church. This was combined with an increasing tendency to see the professional clergy in terms of a renewed Old Testament priesthood, set apart from the rest of the *laos*, especially when it came to the administration of the Lord's Supper. Clement of Rome was the first to use the word *laikos* (laity) in its modern sense; and by the third century Cyprian, Bishop of Carthage, was teaching that clergy were distinct from lay people, and was quite consciously drawing parallels between bishops of the Christian Church and senators of the Roman state.

The Protestant Reformation should have radically reversed this clericalising tendency, but all too often ended up simply replacing the divide between priest and laity with an alternative divide between *preacher* and laity. And despite some hugely welcome theological developments over the past decades—most especially a rediscovery of Paul's powerful image of the body of Christ—today's expression of the Church's desire to 'be like all the other nations' lies in her tendency to adopt secular management models, to centralise power, and to draw analogies with the professional–lay distinctions found in other walks of life.

There is an uncomfortable collusion here which can all

too easily take place between clergy and laity (to use those terms in their usual sense)—for the laity's desire to 'be like all the other nations' and to 'have a king to lead us and to go out before us and fight our battles' can all too easily suit both parties rather well, while remaining disastrous as a means of extending the kingdom of God. On the clergy side, there is something attractive about being thought professional, courageous, holy in a way that distinguishes them from the bulk of the people; and more so when the 'battles' are generally not too arduous provided they purposefully keep their head beneath the cultural parapet. On the laity side, there is something comforting in the idea that someone else might go out and fight the kingdom battles on their behalf; though quite what those battles might be—what the clergy actually spend their time doing—often remains something of a mystery!

In response to the privilege of having this representative who (at the very least) prays for them, pastors them and preaches at them, the laity are happy to assist the clergy, digging (if not especially deeply) into their pockets and sacrificing (if not especially generously) some of the hours they call their 'spare time'. But reverse the process—suggest that the 'clergy' are there to equip the 'laity' to be God's ministers and missioners in their homes and communities and workplaces—and that comfortable collusion is shattered. From the clergy point of view, there's hard work ahead: not just preaching safe little homilies, but seeking to live and proclaim Christ in a way that will motivate a whole generation of ministers and missionaries. From the laity point of view, new vistas open up which are exciting and alarming in equal measure: not just belonging to a club and paying the subscriptions, but seeking first the kingdom of

God, whatever the cost and wherever God takes them. It's no wonder that the 'priesthood of all believers' has proved such a difficult concept for the Church to keep hold of for long.

In the days of Christendom—the era when the Christian faith was generally accepted (in the West at least) as the best foundation for our life together as a family and community and nation—there was less pressure to break free from this debilitating collusion. Clergy would preach to a reasonably large congregation, the congregation would pay their dues, and the whole thing worked, at least on a superficial level. But it isn't working now. Those churches which have failed to recognise the power and dazzling brilliance of the Goliath juggernaut—those fellowships which have tried to perpetuate a system where some 'do' ministry and others have it 'done' to them—are falling by the wayside. Only those churches where the people of God are the ministers and missionaries—where the *laos* is being inspired and equipped to 'seek first the kingdom of God and his righteousness'—are making any kind of progress.

And what of the clergy in this scenario? What of those who may well have acknowledged one half of the Stockdale Paradox—'the discipline to confront the most brutal facts of your current reality, whatever they might be'—but have lost touch with the other half: 'faith that you will prevail in the end'? In many ways, it can leave them in a similar situation to that of King Saul. They may be insecure, even mildly depressive as people. They are almost certainly compromised and, more seriously, may be trying to cover up the extent of that compromise to their congregations, their families and perhaps themselves. But above all, they've been put in an impossible position—they've been set up to fail—as they perpetuate a model of church leadership which was never God's intention from the start.

True, they may still find some lingering measure of respect in their parishes. They may even be accorded some of the honours bestowed on other community leaders. But even the most gifted and godly of ministers are not going to bring in the kingdom of God on their own, with their congregation as the mere recipients of an increasingly ineffective or desperate ministry. In the face of the Goliath of modern-day secularism, and given the inadequate patterns of leadership inherited from the Christendom generations, both Saul and the Israelites *will* end up paralysed, dismayed and terrified. Even evolution is not enough—a cumbersome recruitment of volunteers (perhaps as licensed lay workers) to share the vicar's workload. What is required is nothing short of revolution, reformation, even fundamentalism in the sense of returning to the ministerial fundamentals of the first-generation Church.

Saul, sadly, was not in a position to lead that revolution, though things might have turned out very differently had his compromised conduct led to a genuine repentance rather than the set of feeble excuses trotted out in 1 Samuel 15. While Saul was in charge, God's chosen people would remain God's frozen people, and only with David would the revolution begin. But until we address the deadening effects of a faulty view of leadership—until we genuinely embrace the missionary potential of the whole people of God—the church will lack the confidence to take the fight to Goliath and to make the kind of inroads into our society which are critically required. 'Who could have designed a system,' asks R. Paul Stevens in exasperation, 'by which people can hear two sermons a Sunday for the whole of their lives and not be able to open up the Bible to others publicly?'[13] Whoever designed it, there is no question of the contemporary need to go back to the drawing board.

A new blueprint

'The people of God'; 'the body of Christ': both suggest that the Church is called to be a living, breathing organism, and not primarily a functional and hierarchical organisation. In the local setting, that implies that the unique body of believers who meet to worship on a Sunday morning has been brought together for a purpose. It is not simply there to prop up an organisation, to fulfil the vicar's vision or to construct some identikit church complete with all the trimmings which their particular churchmanship requires of them; it is there rather to develop a Christian community which is as unique in its sum as in its parts.

What visions and passions has God given to this body of believers? What gifts and experiences do they share? What are the areas which fire them up? In my own experience they will be many and varied. In my last parish, for example, the presence of a large abortion clinic 300 yards from the church motivated a small group of people to get praying over this whole vexed issue. Some of the group felt called to train as crisis pregnancy counsellors, while others were drawn to a programme called 'The Journey' for those who had already experienced an abortion. Initially the take-up rate for these services was very low—just a handful of individuals in the first two years—but eventually the team was counselling more than 150 people each year. Off the back of that, a sex-and-relationships package was developed and offered to half a dozen secondary schools in our area. Most of those schools gratefully accepted the offer, so that the majority of the sex-and-relationships teaching in that borough is now offered by wise, caring, praying Christian disciples.

It's just one example, and I could mention many more from nearly three decades of ordained ministry. Over that time I have been privileged to lead churches which have set up Christian nursery schools, prison fellowship groups, church plants, parenting courses, community cafés, football leagues, curry nights and exercise classes for the elderly, and I can safely say that few of those visions originated from me, or formed part of some streamlined, centralised five-year plan. A while back, we experimented with the small groups in our church, asking their leaders to seek a unique vision for their group, then to invite others to come on board. All kinds of groups emerged, around 40 in all: one for medical professionals wrestling with ethical issues from a Christian perspective, another committed to a verse-by-verse exploration of the letter to the Romans, a third focused on the Jewish roots of the Christian faith, and a fourth engaged in a weekly programme of worship, study and knocking on the doors of their neighbours. Most of the groups flourished, since they were populated by people who had prayerfully chosen to do what they were doing. Only the door-knocking team struggled for a while after one of its leaders misheard my encouragement that the group was 'prophetic' and passed on the view that I thought it 'pathetic'!

One of our best sermon series was based on ministry in the workplace. As part of each service, a variety of people stood up to describe something of what it was like to minister as a Christian at Heathrow Airport, the West Middlesex Hospital, GlaxoSmithKline or the City of London. Integrity, ambition, success and failure, rest—all were scrutinised from a scriptural perspective, and never had our church come closer to realising the vision of the 'priesthood of all believers' than during that time.[14]

'Unleashing the church'—in Frank Tillapaugh's memorable phrase[15]—is a risky procedure. While organisations can be neat and tidy, organisms are unpredictable and have a (sometimes awkward) life of their own. The unleashed church, though, is not a chaotic church: it is rather a church which gives precedence to gospel values over specific strategic objectives, a church that seeks to be a sailing ship (directed and empowered by the wind of the Spirit) rather than a bus (stopping off at certain predetermined destinations). It's true that the five-year plan has some value for churches whose vision is beginning to shift from maintenance to mission, but the ultimate goal should be of a community where our sons and daughters prophesy, our young men see visions and our older men dream dreams;[16] a church where all take initiatives (large or small) for the glory of God's name and the extension of his kingdom.

Taking stock

We've come to the end of verse 11 of our Bible chapter, and it's good to take stock of where we've got to in our reflections on godly confidence. We have seen the need to build on the lessons of the past (both the easy lessons and the tougher ones); we have recognised the wisdom of facing the realities of the present (holding on to both sides of the Stockdale Paradox); and we have acknowledged the necessity of shaping up to the challenges of the future (where the reaffirmation of the 'priesthood of all believers' will largely determine the future health, perhaps existence, of the church in the West).

And so we are left with a juggernaut of a Philistine champion, and with a king and his people who are staring at the oncoming headlights, completely unable to move. The stage is set for a young man to burst on to the scene and change everything.

— 4 —

Confidence in the Providence of God: Introducing David

'Do you believe in God?' Grace Davie asked an interviewee in the streets of Islington in the late 1960s. 'Yes,' was the answer.

'Do you believe in a God who can change the course of events on earth?' Davie persisted. 'No,' replied the interviewee, 'just the ordinary one.'[1]

It's a telling exchange, and one which raises a key question both outside and within the church: 'What is our working theology, the worldview by which we actually live our lives?' Davie's interviewee was representative of a large swathe of the British population who happily tick the 'Christian' or 'Church of England' box when faced with surveys and questionnaires, but whose view of God is poles apart from anything that resembles traditional Christian belief. The idea of a God who intervenes in human history, a God of creation, salvation and providence, a God who heals and strengthens, who guides and equips, a 'living God', is far removed from both the experience and the expectation of such people; and though most of them remain outside the walls of any church, there are others who take their place in the pews Sunday by Sunday, reciting a creed and singing faith-filled hymns which bear very little resemblance to the way they live, think or behave. Indeed, few Christians are completely immune from such a tendency.

There are three books on my bookshelves with similar titles: first, J.B. Phillips' classic *Your God Is Too Small*, which deconstructed many prevalent views of God in the early 1950s (the Resident Policeman, the Parental Hangover, the Grand Old Man, the Pale Galilean) before providing a more constructive alternative view; next, John Young's *Our God Is Still Too Small*, which updated Phillips' approach for the 1980s, this time taking on the Lucky Charm God, the Odd Job God, the Killjoy God and the Silent God; and finally, Bruce Ware's *Their God Is Too Small*, a rather more academic treatise exposing the loving but essentially impotent god of the so-called open theists.[2] The idea of writing books whose titles include the words 'God' and 'too small' may well have had its day—but perhaps there is a need for prophets in every generation to challenge the idolatries of their time, rescuing even Christian people from an impoverished view of God which will only lead to growing disillusionment and a loss of faith, hope and godly confidence.

How would Saul and his army have responded to Grace Davie's questions, had a similar researcher been investigating the state of religion in the Israel of their day? Clearly they would have given a resounding 'yes' to the first question, but the second—'Do you believe in a God who can change the course of events on earth?'—would have found them far more tentative. And that is where our story takes a decisive turn with the arrival of a young shepherd boy on to the battlefield, picnic hamper in hand, who sees what the Israelites are seeing and hears what they are hearing, but whose God is a whole lot bigger than their God.

A fresh perspective

Now David was the son of an Ephrathite named Jesse, who was from Bethlehem in Judah. Jesse had eight sons, and in Saul's time he was very old. Jesse's three eldest sons had followed Saul to the war: the firstborn was Eliab; the second, Abinadab; and the third, Shammah. David was the youngest. The three eldest followed Saul, but David went back and forth from Saul to tend his father's sheep at Bethlehem.

For forty days the Philistine came forward every morning and evening and took his stand.

Now Jesse said to his son David, 'Take this ephah of roasted grain and these ten loaves of bread for your brothers and hurry to their camp. Take along these ten cheeses to the commander of their unit. See how your brothers are and bring back some assurance from them. They are with Saul and all the men of Israel in the Valley of Elah, fighting against the Philistines.'

Early in the morning David left the flock in the care of a shepherd, loaded up and set out, as Jesse had directed. He reached the camp as the army was going out to its battle positions, shouting the war cry. Israel and the Philistines were drawing up their lines facing each other. David left his things with the keeper of supplies, ran to the battle lines and asked his brothers how they were. As he was talking with them, Goliath, the Philistine champion from Gath, stepped out from his lines and shouted his usual defiance, and David heard it. When the Israelites saw the man, they all fled from him in great fear.

Now the Israelites had been saying, 'Do you see how this man keeps coming out? He comes out to defy Israel. The king will give great wealth to the man who kills him. He will also give him his daughter in marriage and will exempt his family line from taxes in Israel.'

David asked those standing near him, 'What will be done for the man who kills this Philistine and removes this disgrace from Israel? Who is this uncircumcised Philistine that he should defy the armies of the living God?'

They repeated to him what they had been saying and told him, 'This is what will be done for the man who kills him.'

1 SAMUEL 17:12–27

Saul had his date with destiny while chasing donkeys across the Israelite countryside; for David it happened on a cheese-delivery run. And there is something about the sheer ordinariness of these verses which is curiously compelling. In the first chapter of Luke's Gospel, Zechariah's encounter with God took place at the high point of his priestly career, the once-in-a-lifetime moment when he was chosen by lot to offer incense in the inner court of the Jerusalem temple.[3] But his story is the exception, not the rule in the history of salvation. Far more commonly, a man or woman wakes up in the morning with very little on their minds beyond the mundane work of the day ahead; yet by the end of the day something has happened which will change the course of their lives for ever.

Perhaps it was the apparently trivial nature of these verses, and the leisurely pace at which David is introduced, which led to their omission in the shorter text of the Septuagint: the translators were probably anxious to get on with the story.[4] But whatever their motivation, they missed a treat. For the comparison between Goliath the bombastic bully and David, the shepherd and messenger boy, is brilliantly drawn in this passage, the details of roasted grain and loaves and cheeses contrasting (hardly impressively) with the similarly detailed earlier account of helmets and javelins and spear shafts 'like a weaver's rod'.

David's older brothers have some significance in this passage: to their father Jesse, they were 'with Saul and all the men of Israel in the Valley of Elah, fighting the Philistines' (v. 19, which, given our prior knowledge of the real situation, was little more than wishful thinking!). But David himself was at his father's beck and call, shuttling back and forth from the fields to home to the battlefront to home again. Even the biographical note, which reminds us that Jesse had eight sons and that David was the youngest, seems deliberately inserted to emphasise the unremarkable nature of this boy. In Hebrew numerology seven was the number of perfection, so the eighth son might well have been considered something of an afterthought, the runt of the family. Indeed, the Hebrew word for the youngest son, *haqqaton*, has just this disparaging runt-like quality.[5]

It's a perception which is fleshed out in an earlier introduction to young David—for 1 Samuel 16 presents us with the familiar story of Samuel seeking out a new king for Israel and working his way through the seven older sons from Eliab downwards (vv. 5–10). As each candidate received the divine thumbs-down, Samuel asked in some bewilderment, 'Are these all the sons you have?' 'No,' was Jesse's reply. 'There is still the youngest. He is tending the sheep' (v. 11). The very fact that Jesse had not previously thought to invite David to attend the solemn act of consecration in the presence of the mighty Samuel speaks volumes about his somewhat negative attitude towards son number perfection-plus-one. There's something of the Cinderella in the story of this young shepherd boy.

1 Samuel 16, then, introduces David as a youngest son, a shepherd boy, and a man anointed as king by Samuel and empowered by the Spirit of the Lord. It goes on to recount the story of Saul's emotional turmoil, and to present us with evidence of David's more sensitive and aesthetic side. Earlier in the chapter, Samuel had been instructed that 'the Lord does not look at the things human beings look at. People look at the outward appearance, but the Lord looks at the heart' (v. 7);[6] yet even then our narrator can't steer clear of a reference to David's fine appearance and handsome features (v. 12)! As if that's not enough, no one could wish for a better reference than that given by one of Saul's servants in verse 18: 'I have seen a son of Jesse of Bethlehem who knows how to play the harp. He is a brave man and a warrior. He speaks well and is a fine-looking man. And the Lord is with him.' It's hardly surprising that by the end of the chapter, for the first (and almost the last) time, 'Saul liked him very much' (v. 21).

A great deal has been written to explore the relationship between the David of 1 Samuel 16 and the David who appears on the scene in 1 Samuel 17, since the latter chapter seems to present our young hero as if for the first time. It could well be that the narrator was working from several sources, or that he reintroduced David as a matter of narrative technique: as Robert Gordon puts it, 'Stories told in the folkloristic mode sometimes reflect the view that a hero is more of a hero if he is an outsider.'[7] But the fact that we already have some inside knowledge about this outsider in no way detracts from the humble role in which he is now engaged.

It was a role which he may have carried out on several previous occasions—bringing provisions to his brothers and news back to his father—and we can only assume that David was one among hundreds of younger people engaged in similar support for the men on the front line. But this time it was different. David, it seems, had set off exceptionally early in the morning and so was there to witness the start of the day's hostilities, an opportunity he accepted with relish.[8] Israel and the Philistines drew up their battle lines, facing one another. Both armies shouted out their battle cries. So far, so predictable. But then Goliath stepped forward, bellowing out his derisive taunts, and the result was the same pathetic response as that of the past 40 days. Whatever the impression previously given by his older brothers (an impression which had presumably led Jesse to believe that the fight was on), the reality was that 'whenever the Israelites saw the man, they all fled from him in great fear' (v. 24).

By this stage Saul was getting desperate. Like a ruler in one of our fairy stories, he'd offered great wealth to anyone who killed Goliath, along with an enticing tax break and the hand of one of his daughters in marriage. Whether that last promise was a positive one may be open to question: David was later to find Saul's daughter Michal a real handful, and Saul, his future father-in-law, more of a handful still! But the fear that had seized both Saul and his troops—a panic reminiscent of that of the Philistines a few chapters earlier—means that his offer was unlikely to be taken up. Saul's money seemed safe, and Michal and her sisters remained firmly on the marriage market.

As David set his eyes on Goliath, he, like his compatriots, saw a juggernaut of a man, protected by a mass of hard-core armour and weaponry—an Achilles, a Hector. Yet from the start David's perspective was quite different from theirs. It's not that his motivation in quizzing his fellow Israelites was purely selfless: his very first response, in effect, was to ask what was in it for him! But any sense that this Philistine represented an invincible threat to the people of God was immediately dismissed in two of those rhetorical flourishes in which young David specialised: 'What will be done for the man who kills this Philistine and removes this disgrace from Israel?' and 'Who is this uncircumcised Philistine that he should defy the armies of the living God?'

Up to this point we have heard the name of this giant from Gath on three separate occasions: he was Goliath, the Philistine champion, and the very name struck terror into the hearts of every Israelite soldier. But David never used his name—not once. He simply called him 'this Philistine' or else 'this uncircumcised Philistine' or even 'this disgrace', later comparing the threat he posed to that of a lion or bear (v. 37). The reference to circumcision is a particularly interesting one, for at a time when both Israel and most of her Canaanite neighbours practised circumcision, David's jibe may have been as political as it was religious. The question 'Who is this uncircumcised Philistine?' certainly raises issues of holiness, cleanliness and obedience to the true God; but it also reminded David's listeners that the Philistines were foreigners in the land of Canaan—Greek not Semitic—that they simply didn't belong.

It's not just that David stopped using Goliath's name, though. It's also that he started using the name of God: both the holy name Yahweh (or Lord), which had been revealed to Moses as he stood before the burning bush in that defining moment in Israel's history (v. 37; see Exodus 3:14–15); but also, more specifically, that powerful phrase, 'the *living* God'. The name of Goliath had been on the lips of every soldier in the Israelite army, but before David's questions in verse 26 there had been no mention of God at all. The 'rabbits', their eyes blinded by the dazzling sight of the Goliath juggernaut, had allowed Yahweh to slip from the picture altogether.

The living God

For readers who decide to work their way through the Bible from beginning to end, this phrase the 'living God' will become very familiar by the time they get to the prophets and into the New Testament; but up until the events of 1 Samuel 17 it is found on just two occasions, both of them events of the greatest significance. Moses posed his own rhetorical question following his proclamation of the Ten Commandments in Deuteronomy 5: 'What mortal has ever heard the voice of the living God speaking out of fire, as we have, and survived?' (v. 26); while Joshua, standing on the banks of the Jordan River, told his people, 'This is how you will know that the living God is among you... As soon as the priests who carry the ark of the Lord... set foot in the Jordan, its waters flowing downstream will be cut off and stand up in a heap' (Joshua 3:10, 13).

There are certain defining moments in the history of Israel, in other words, in which this phrase occurs: the giving of the law, the possession of the land, and now the establishment of David as rightful king of Israel. And with Goliath reduced to an uncircumcised Philistine, a disgrace, a beast; with the Lord acknowledged and magnified as the living God; with Goliath's defiance reclassified not simply as a defiance of the ranks of Israel but as a stand against the armies of that living God, the balance of the story begins to shift.

In one sense, nothing had changed. The Israelites were

still paralysed. Saul, their king, was still weak and confused. Goliath was still there, all nine foot of him (or six foot nine, according to the Septuagint!). The only change was that Israel now had a leader in her midst: anointed, Spirit-filled, a man who was prepared to speak, to act, even to put his life on the line for the sake of the living God.

The ordinary and the extraordinary

The 1960s Islington resident who answered Grace Davie's questions may not have known it, but her 'ordinary' God was in fact the non-interventionist god of the deists. As a philosophical movement, deism flourished in Britain, France and the United States in the 17th and 18th centuries, forming a middle way between a robust biblical faith on the one hand and a full-blown atheism on the other; and though most of its proponents are now largely forgotten, it continues to exert a major influence on popular thought, allowing people to claim some Christian affiliation while rejecting any sense that God might intervene in their lives or in the world around them.

Even within the church, it is not unusual to come across deist tendencies: a stated belief in God combined with a total lack of expectation as to his continuing presence and activity. Writing of his own denomination, Kirk Bottomley, an American Presbyterian minister, claims:

If they knew what a deist was, many Presbyterians would check that box. For them, God has wound up the Universe like a great clock, and it is more or less ticking away on its own… I do not pretend to defend this position: it is unbiblical and unchristian. But you find it all over the American church scene, especially in mainline churches such as mine, espoused by pastors and laypeople alike.[9]

To speak of confidence in such a God makes no sense at all.

In reaction to this position there have been a number of movements in the past hundred years placing special emphasis on the extraordinary God. The story of Pentecostalism (described by Harvard theologian Harvey Cox as 'a spiritual hurricane which has already touched half a billion people')[10] began in the early days of the 20th century, and is particularly associated with services held at Azusa Street, Los Angeles—meetings which were characterised by speaking in tongues, healing miracles, interracial mingling and (most shocking of all) 'physical demonstrations of emotion'! More than 50 years later, Dennis Bennett, rector of an Episcopalian church in California, astonished his congregation (and infuriated his bishop) with the news that he too had been filled with the Spirit and had spoken in tongues; and Bennett's bestseller *Nine O'clock in the Morning* (new edn. Bridge Publishing, 1994) helped pave the way for those in more mainline denominations to embrace the insights of the renewal movement. Anglican vicar David Watson and Vineyard pastor John Wimber were especially influential in developing those insights in the British context; and, in the words of Alister McGrath, '[The movement's] sense of the immediacy of God's presence through the Holy Spirit is of potentially immense importance in repairing the felt loss of the presence of the divine in everyday life in the West'.[11]

Returning to 1 Samuel 17, there is no question as to the relative positions of Saul and David in regard to this particular theological fence. Both men theoretically shared the same religion: they believed in the God of Abraham, Isaac and Jacob; they celebrated the Passover, and all that God achieved under Moses and Joshua; they knew the Ten Commandments, and could probably recite large chunks of the Law by heart. They had the same scriptures, they sang the same hymns, they listened to the same sermons. Yet Saul and his army, fleeing from the sight and sound of Goliath, were proto-deists, while David, with his talk of the 'living God' (along with actions which matched his rhetoric) was a proto-Pentecostal. The only sadness (and it's a sadness replicated in the lives of many church members and leaders today) is that Saul began his ministry on the 'Pentecostal' side of the fence before life became complicated and compromised. 'Is Saul also among the prophets?' was the question asked of him in his earlier life, as the Spirit of God came upon him in power (1 Samuel 10:9–11). Seven chapters on, had the question been posed once again, the answer would have been a resounding 'No'.[12]

'Your God is too small' is therefore a challenge to be addressed not simply to those outside the people of God, but those inside too—to every Christian believer who from time to time succumbs to the dreary yet unthreatening charms of a deist position. Paul makes that point as he urges the Christians in Thessalonica, 'Do not put out the Spirit's fire. Do not treat prophecies with contempt but test them all; hold on to what is good, reject whatever is harmful' (1 Thessalonians 5:19–22; see also Hebrews 3:12). Keep hold of your confidence, as he might have put it—a confidence in the living God.

It's comparatively easy to take pot shots at the deists. But there's also a sense that even the God of the Pentecostals can become too small: that the very emphasis on the extraordinary—on miracles, signs and wonders—can blind us to the activity of the living God in the ordinariness of our lives.

I remember my first experience of Pentecostal worship in a large black-majority church in Lewisham, south-east London. The service lasted about three hours, combining fiery preaching, passionate praying and glorious singing, and was an almost overwhelming experience. What struck me most, though, was the amount of time given to what were described as 'testimonies', frequently moving accounts of how God had interacted in the lives of members of the congregation. From my own evangelical perspective, a testimony was a well-prepared explanation of how I had become a Christian, not the most dramatic of stories (in my case), and one which was already at least ten years old. For these people, though, a testimony was far more fresh and immediate, speaking of events that had taken place entirely in the past couple of weeks. And it wasn't that those events were trouble-free or dramatic: many of the stories spoke of God's presence in the face of heart-breaking poverty, racism, sickness and bereavement. But there was an extraordinary alertness both to the power of a miraculous God and to the providence of a faithful God—a sense, in the terms of Romans 8, that 'in all things God works for the good of those who love him, who have been called according to his purpose' (v. 28), and that '[nothing] will be able to separate us from the love of God that is in Christ Jesus our Lord' (v. 39).

That was my experience in the early 1980s, an encounter which perfectly matched the confidence of young David in the face of the most alarming of the Philistines. But in the intervening years I have frequently come across a less helpful trend within Pentecostal and charismatic circles—a tendency for the God of the ordinary to be so supplanted by the God of the extraordinary that our faith becomes dependent on a regular diet of healings, signs and wonders for its very survival. We become miracle junkies, with our levels of confidence dropping sharply between 'fixes' (and with those 'fixes' themselves remaining entirely outside our control).

It's not that extraordinary things don't happen: I myself have been privileged to witness a number of divine interventions which are quite inexplicable from a purely rationalist standpoint.[13] But a faith which is rooted in such occurrences will always be fragile, unable to withstand the chill winds of discouragement, suffering, persecution and the long, hard grind. 'Unless you people see signs and wonders, you will never believe,' said Jesus of this tendency (John 4:48), while the author of the letter to the Hebrews reminded his readers that 'faith is being sure of what we hope for and certain of what we do not see' (11:1).

'Your God is too small.' It's an absolutely clear-cut charge to be made against the deists of our day, but to bring the self-same accusation against some Pentecostals and their charismatic cousins seems odd and unfair. Yet the bigness of the living God embraces far more than the miraculous: it takes in creation and salvation, suffering and healing, death and resurrection, the call to evangelism and the call to social action. A robust doctrine of God's providence—his personal care for the creation he has made, rather than the mechanistic and self-centred 'providence' of the deists[14]—puts the 'awe' back into 'ordinary'. It encourages us to proclaim with Julian of Norwich that 'all shall be well, and all shall be well, and all manner of things shall be well'.[15] It enables us to sing with Nahum Tate (1652–1715) and Nicholas Brady (1659–1726):

Through all the changing scenes of life,
In trouble and in joy,
The praises of my God shall still
My heart and tongue employ.

Such a faith may not look too flashy or impressive. It may lack the drama and pizzazz of the TV evangelist or travelling miracle-worker. It may seem confusing compared with the more simplistic messages of the deists ('miracles never happen') or their Pentecostal opponents ('miracles always happen'). But where we remain alert both to the power of a miraculous God and to the providence of a faithful God, our faith will be unstoppable and our confidence unquenchable. As Jesus' metaphor of the mustard seed reminds us, it's not the size of our faith that counts; it is rather the size of the one in whom our faith is placed (Matthew 17:20).

There is, after all, no clear miracle in 1 Samuel 17, unless it lies in Goliath's massive dimensions. On one level this is simply the story of a young man outsmarting his larger and more experienced opponent. Nor is the rest of the story of David liberally scattered with signs and wonders; in fact, they hardly feature at all. And it's not that the miraculous is unimportant or irrelevant: indeed, belief in the living God *must* encompass a belief in, even an expectation of, 'signs and wonders'. But the sense that God is *only* at work at such times—that all healings, for example, must be demonstrably miraculous before we attribute them to God—does no justice to his creation or providence, his ongoing presence and activity, to the Lord as our Shepherd. Instead it tends towards a theology of the 'God of the gaps', which rests on an entirely unbiblical division between the natural and the supernatural, and which reluctantly gives God the credit only when every conceivable alternative explanation has been fully explored and exhausted. And what better way—especially at those times when miracles are thin on the ground—to play into the hands of the deists and their atheistic cousins?

Rediscovering the providence of God

The story of David in these verses is, as we have seen, an ordinary story of a young man with a picnic basket. It is equally an extraordinary story of a God who directs, inspires, motivates and releases his people from the paralysis into which their faithlessness, their proto-deism, has led them. A little later in the chapter we read of how David had killed both lions and bears (17:36), while in the very next verse it is *the Lord* who had delivered him from their paws. To whom, then, did those animals owe their untimely end? The doctrine of God's providence can construe the same event as both an act of David and an act of God, enabling us to interpret its full significance from both a human and a divine perspective.

For Christians, too, our belief in God's providence has even stronger foundations. As Kathryn Tanner writes in her reflections on the theology of Karl Barth:

Understanding both God and creatures in Christ, [we] can be assured that the world is a place where God's mercy, wisdom and goodness finally reign. Only in Christ is it sure that the world will be preserved, that God works in it for the creatures' good, and that forces of chaos and destruction will not triumph over it.[16]

That doesn't excuse us from taking seriously the second part of the Stockdale Paradox—the 'discipline to confront the most brutal facts of your current reality, whatever they might be'; nor does it stop us periodically joining in with the exasperated prayer of Desmond Tutu, 'For goodness' sake, why don't You make it more obvious that *You are* in charge?'[17] But it does place that discipline and that prayer in the context of the first part of the paradox, the 'faith that you will prevail in the end'.

Reviewing our lives in a spirit of thankfulness—recognising the presence of the living God in both the ordinary and the extraordinary—is foundational to a life which is hopeful, cheerful and confident. A faith which is built on the rhetorical questioning of a David ('Who is this uncircumcised Philistine that he should defy the armies of the living God?' 1 Samuel 17:26) or a Paul ('If God is for us, who can be against us?' Romans 8:31) is a faith that means business, a faith that gets things done.

It's true that most Christians (myself included) will confess to times when such confidence is a long way from our experience, when the Goliaths that confront us make us want to retreat, even to flee in fear. It's true that there can be a yawning gap between our professed beliefs and the worldview by which we actually live. But to settle permanently in the land of the deists—to allow our understanding of God to become so enfeebled, so impotent, so irrelevant to any aspect of our day-to-day living—is a terrible mistake. David never used the phrase 'the living God' in his confrontation with Goliath the Philistine. He only used it when addressing Saul's army and Saul himself. For while the world's understanding of God might well be muddled, superstitious, gullible and contradictory, it is often God's people and their leaders who need to be challenged with the simple message, 'Your God is too small'.

— 5 —

Responding to Godly Confidence: Eliab, Saul and David

It was George Verwer, founder of the international mission organisation 'Operation Mobilisation', who famously said, 'It's easier to cool down a fanatic than to warm up a corpse'; and his words have returned to me on many occasions, most commonly when interviewing for clergy posts. Corpses, in Verwer's sense, represent very little threat to the established order: they are dignified and respectful, they willingly fit into the box that we create for them, they never raise their voices or bring up awkward questions, and their very lack of enthusiasm, warmth and passion is somehow comforting, feeding the illusion that my own faith is doing pretty well, and thank you for asking! Fanatics are far more alarming: zealous, wild-eyed, with scary tales of the living God and a fervent desire to see his name honoured and his kingdom extended, the fanatic is in turn challenging, disturbing, awkward, embarrassing; and frequently, one suspects, just what the doctor ordered.

It's not that the fanatic is always right, or that lessons of tact and discretion are somehow unimportant: an unteachable fanatic is unquestionably a nightmare. But years of experience have taught me that the first qualification for any Christian worker is not their ability to tick every box (with commendable neatness) on the job description and person spec. It is rather that indefinable but easily recognisable trait we call a 'fire in their belly'.

Over the years this passionate confidence in the living God has not been highly valued in the denomination of which I am a part (the Church of England). In the middle of the 18th century Bishop Butler famously remarked to John Wesley, 'Sir, the pretending to extraordinary revelations and gifts of the Holy Spirit is a horrid thing, a very horrid thing';[1] and while few would use Bishop Butler's terminology today, far more would share his wariness of anything approaching religious enthusiasm. The people most likely to be turned down by clergy selection panels (up until the last few years, at least) have not, in my experience, been the mild-mannered or the dithering. They have rather been the confident and self-assured. The leaders most likely to have a tough time through the course of their ministry have not been the little people, with small and unassuming ambitions for the churches they lead. They have been the big people, the very scale of whose vision has inspired and alarmed in roughly equal measure.

In more recent times there has been a discernible shift in the church's thinking in this area, as the scale of the Goliath that confronts us has become increasingly evident. As part of that shift, the word 'confidence' is being reinstated as a positive quality rather than as a synonym of the word 'arrogance';[2] bold appointments (and not mere 'safe pairs of hands') are being made to key positions in the church; young ordinands are being recruited once again, following decades in which the church pursued the suicidal policy of turning away youthful 'fanatics' rather than seeking to channel their passion in positive directions; and the report *Mission-Shaped Church* (CHP, 2000), together with the recent 'Reform and

Renewal' programme, have helped to encourage a pioneering approach to ministry far more akin to the boldness of a David than to the paralysis of his fear-filled compatriots. Perhaps these changes are in part born out of desperation, but they are hugely welcome nonetheless. Indeed, desperation—a crying out to the Lord in the face of overwhelming odds—is an infinitely godlier characteristic than the deadening complacency that remains the default setting of a church that has lost its way.

How do we respond to the 'fanatics', the big people, in our midst? That is the question at the heart of the story of Eliab and Saul as they reacted to young David and his fighting talk of uncircumcised Philistines and the living God. On this occasion, as we shall see, it was Saul who came up trumps—Saul who allowed the intensity of the fire in David's belly to reawaken the fire in his own. Yet Eliab's response is also instructive: the cynical approach of a man who has seen and done it all, and who makes it his mission not simply to cool but to smother the fire of faith within the runt of the family, brother number perfection-plus-one.

Cynicism and the dawning of belief

When Eliab, David's eldest brother, heard him speaking with the men, he burned with anger at him and asked, 'Why have you come down here? And with whom did you leave those few sheep in the wilderness? I know how conceited you are and how wicked your heart is; you came down only to watch the battle.'

'Now what have I done?' said David. 'Can't I even speak?' He then turned away to someone else and brought up the same matter, and the men answered him as before. What David said was overheard and reported to Saul, and Saul sent for him.

David said to Saul, 'Let no one lose heart on account of this Philistine; your servant will go and fight him.'

Saul replied, 'You are not able to go out against this Philistine and fight him; you are little more than a boy, and he has been a warrior from his youth.'

But David said to Saul, 'Your servant has been keeping his father's sheep. When a lion or a bear came and carried off a sheep from the flock, I went after it, struck it and rescued the sheep from its mouth. When it turned on me, I seized it by its hair, struck it and killed it. Your servant has killed both the lion and the bear; this uncircumcised Philistine will be like one of them, because he has defied the armies of the living God. The Lord who rescued me from the paw of the lion and the paw of the bear will rescue me from the hand of this Philistine.'

Saul said to David, 'Go, and the Lord be with you.'

1 SAMUEL 17:28–37

From the moment when sin first crouched at a young man's door and threatened to overpower him (Genesis 4:7), the biblical accounts of sibling relationships are fraught with difficulties. Cain killed Abel, Jacob cheated Esau, and Joseph's brothers threw him into a pit before selling him into slavery. Jesus' own brothers[3] joined the disciples for prayer in the weeks leading up to the Day of Pentecost (Acts 1:14), and one of them, James, ended up leading the church in Jerusalem. But previously there were times when they 'did not believe in him' (John 7:5), and at least one occasion when they considered him 'out of his mind' (Mark 3:21). In fact, the stories of Joseph in the Old Testament and Jesus in the New relate precisely to this question of how we respond to big people, to those whose vision makes them stand out in their family, their community and their generation.

David's brother Eliab was the man who had first caught the eye of Samuel as—like the magi a thousand years later—the prophet arrived in Bethlehem in search of a king (1 Samuel 16:6–7). Not only was Eliab the oldest of Jesse's sons, but he was also tall and well-built, qualities which he shared with the first king of Israel, King Saul. 'Surely the Lord's anointed stands here before the Lord', was Samuel's first response, only to be told in no uncertain terms, 'Do not consider his appearance or his height, for I have rejected him.'

Reading 1 Samuel 17 in the light of this prior event, it was perhaps that sense of rejection and David's subsequent anointing as king 'in the presence of his brothers' (16:13) which fuelled Eliab's angry response to his younger sibling. The parallel with the story of Joseph is all too clear, with both accounts comprising an explosive cocktail of cocky younger brothers, jealous older brothers and an apparently irrational favouritism which honoured the younger above the older. Yet this time the father figure was not some foolish old man bequeathing a special coat to his favourite son: it was none other than God himself, through his prophet Samuel, who had overruled both Jesse and Samuel in his rejection of Eliab the soldier, in favour of David the shepherd boy.

Eliab had further cause to resent his younger brother's arrival on the scene. It is both frightening and frustrating to be paralysed, unable to move in the face of an oncoming juggernaut; and 40 days of Goliath's bombastic taunting had no doubt taken their toll on the morale of all the fighting sons of Jesse, and on that of the entire Israelite army. For David to appear and start talking the language of the 'living God'; for a conversation to be initiated about rewards and tax exemptions and the hand of the king's daughter in marriage, was therefore extremely hard to stomach. 'Why have you come down here?' was Eliab's initial salvo. 'And with whom did you leave those few sheep in the wilderness?' (deliberately playing down David's credentials as a shepherd, let alone a potential giant-slayer). 'I know how conceited you are and how wicked your heart is; you came down only to watch the battle.'

It is interesting how Eliab mentions David's heart at this point—a heart which, in his older brother's view, was conceited, wicked and deceitful. In the previous chapter it was Eliab's own heart, and that of six of his brothers, which had been weighed in the balance and found wanting. But now Eliab takes it on himself to judge the state of David's heart and to misread the younger man's confidence as wickedness and conceit. It's not that David's heart (his inner life) was entirely blameless, of course: the young shepherd's tendency to bring up the subject of rewards amid his glorious rhetoric about the living God reveals him as an all-too-fallible hero, an impression which continued to dog him throughout his future career. But there was something about David's heart, with its rich combination of passion, faith and courage, which singled him out in the Israel of his day. Indeed, of no other Old Testament character does the Lord say that he is 'a man after his own heart' (1 Samuel 13:14).[4]

If Eliab's response to his younger brother was motivated by anger and frustration, Saul's approach was rather more circumspect. What struck him first was the most self-evident of observations, for those who judge by outward appearances at least: the almost laughable contrast in terms of age, bulk and fighting experience between young David and the giant of a man on the other side of the valley. But while Eliab's reply effectively shut David up, Saul's willingness to keep the conversation alive opened up the way to new insights and perspectives which a hundred Eliabs would never have unearthed. In the face of David's confidence, Eliab prejudged and Saul listened.

It was David's testimony which acted as a powerful catalyst to Saul, enabling the king to begin to see the situation through David's eyes and to reconnect with the mighty name of Yahweh. David spoke politely, referring to himself as Saul's servant, and his simple story of fighting off lions and bears was both well-crafted and inspiring. If God had protected him (along with Jesse's flock) from the ravages of those animals on the Bethlehem hillside, how much more would God protect him (along with the Lord's own flock) from this 'uncircumcised Philistine' who had dared to defy the 'armies of the living God'!

David's private battles out on the hillside formed the theme of his speech to Saul. This new battle would be fought in the full glare of the public spotlight. But Saul was wise enough to recognise the importance of the private battle and to acknowledge how David's experience in one field (as a shepherd) was highly relevant to his potential in another (as a giant-killer). It's true, as we shall see, that Saul only partially understood the radical nature of this young fanatic's faith; yet as David speaks we can almost feel the fire returning to Saul's heart. Back in chapter 15, when Saul had ducked and dived in response to Samuel's ruthless questioning, the king had eventually used the sad phrase 'The Lord *your* God' (v. 15) in his conversation with the prophet, poignantly expressing the sense of distance he felt from the God of his forefathers. Here (temporarily at least), the king was back on track once more as he turned to the young shepherd boy and handed him his great commission: 'Go, and the Lord be with you.'

The Eliab reaction

Fear, frustration, jealousy, competitiveness—any (or all) of these qualities can lie behind the Eliab reaction, a response which is all too familiar to the Davids of every generation. Within families, churches and communities we might expect a deeper sense that we're all playing for the same team, and so a greater appreciation of the gifts, passions and enthusiasms of our fellow players; yet even a crisis of the magnitude of Goliath can sometimes fail to engender that team spirit among us, or to dispel the tendency (in the British psyche at least) to equate confidence with arrogance.

I'll never forget a talk I heard given by the leader of one of the then largest and most dynamic churches in the UK. The man spoke movingly but graciously about his own experience of the 'Eliab response' from his colleagues and those in authority over him—the deep suspicion that dogged his every move; and there was no trace of self-pity in what he said or the way he said it, but there was genuine sorrow. And as someone who, myself, had periodically envied the charisma of this man (for I am certainly not immune from the Eliab reaction myself), the talk was a salutary and humbling experience. While Jesus frequently agonised over 'you of little faith' (see Matthew 6:30; 8:26; 16:8), the talk helped me recognise the far more common predisposition in Jesus' church: a tendency to *affirm* 'you of little faith' (the 'corpses' in George Verwer's terms) and to reserve our deepest antipathy for 'you of mammoth faith' (the 'fanatics').

It's a tendency which couldn't be further removed from the Gospels, where Jesus prized faith so highly that he was willing to build his church not on the safe pair of hands of Matthew the accountant or Thomas the realist or even John the beloved, but on Peter, a man of transparent enthusiasm who shared David's awareness of the 'living God' but could also display the most alarming immaturity (see Matthew 16:15–23). In Jesus' parable of the talents, it was the 'fanatics' who got to work, risking all of the money entrusted to them so as to get a good return—while the 'corpse' chose instead to bury the money (for corpses and burials belong together), thus earning for himself not the congratulation of a risk-averse employer but a string of adjectives of which 'lazy' and 'wicked' were the kindest (Matthew 25:14–30). The appointment of Simon the Zealot as one of Jesus' disciples was perhaps the most dramatic example of his commitment to cooling down fanatics rather than warming up corpses; having a potential terrorist on your team must have been a constant challenge, especially as he daily broke bread with Matthew the Roman collaborator. And though Jesus consistently rejected the deadly fanaticism of the Zealot movement, he reserved still stronger condemnation for the 'safe' people of his day, the Pharisees and Sadducees (incidentally describing the former as 'whitewashed tombs... full of the bones of the dead': Matthew 23:27), whose guardianship of the Law and the temple was carried out with the greatest possible tidiness and the smallest possible grace.[5]

Where does this Eliab tendency come from? Why, when Paul instructs God's people to 'rejoice with those who rejoice' and to 'weep with those who weep' (Romans 12:15, RSV), do we frequently find ourselves doing precisely the opposite, quietly rejoicing when others are brought down a peg or two and 'weeping' when they succeed? It's true that the English language doesn't have a term for this dubious attribute, and that we have to borrow a German word, *Schadenfreude*, with which to describe it. But no one looking at today's media (the broadsheets as much as the tabloids) can doubt the extent of the disease in today's society; and belonging to the body of Christ does not provide complete protection from its deadening clutches.

For several years I worked with a colleague (we'll call him Frank) who struggled with the Eliab tendency himself and gave me some insight into its possible roots. Frank told me of an occasion from his early years when his sister had held a birthday party and invited a large number of her friends along. The two of them had had an argument earlier that afternoon, and his sister had made it quite clear that she didn't want Frank to come to her party. So as the games were being played, and the food was being eaten and the cake cut, Frank sat halfway up the stairs, excluded from the celebrations by a door which remained firmly shut in his face.

Not only was the memory so vivid and emotionally charged that Frank found it hard to tell the story 50 years on without tears springing to his eyes; but that picture of a young boy excluded from the action had also become something of a defining image in his life. Somehow, for Frank, the party was always in the other room; it was always other people who were having all the fun. It was a perception which gave Frank a tremendous compassion for those who similarly felt on the outside. But it also made it difficult for him to affirm the confidence of others without hearing in that confidence the shrieks of delight on the other side of the door.

My suspicion is that Frank is not unique, and that the confidence and success of other Christian believers, far from acting as an encouragement to us, can all too easily echo the laughter in the other room and emphasise the loneliness of the stairs. It's not that we'll always admit to others (or even to ourselves) that that is what is happening: it's far easier to mock the naivety of confident Christians, to challenge their motivation, to question their effectiveness, to accuse them of fanaticism, fundamentalism and triumphalism, to ignore them or shut them up with clever phrases learnt at the school of Eliab! But such an approach, while superficially appealing, is potentially devastating to our own spiritual lives and the life of the church as a whole. To close down the conversation with the Davids of our day is a recipe for paralysis and disillusionment, as Goliath remains enthroned and the language of growth is replaced by the language of 'managed decline'.

Perhaps it is unsurprising in such a context to discover that younger, less experienced leaders are often better at leading growing churches than those who are older and allegedly wiser, one of the intriguing statistics revealed in Bob Jackson's research for the Church of England.[6] These younger clergy are more likely to share the passionate faith of a David, and less likely to have been tainted by the world-weary cynicism of an Eliab. There may be nothing especially startling about these findings, but they do represent a dual challenge to the church: not simply 'How do we stop the Eliabs quenching the fire of the Davids?' but also, 'How do we allow the fire of the Davids to fan into flame the dying embers of the Eliabs?'

Fanning the embers

Once given the chance of a hearing, as we have seen, young David spoke with great sensitivity and maturity in a way that reawakened faith in Saul. His was not a triumphalistic speech or one marked with a sense of superiority or arrogance.

Instead he expressed a proper position of humility before his king, and spoke of lions and bears and of his own God-given abilities of strength and courage. A thousand years later, Paul wrote to Timothy, one of the younger leaders of the church in Ephesus, and instructed him: 'Don't let anyone look down on you because you are young, but set an example for the believers in speech, in conduct, in love, in faith and in purity' (1 Timothy 4:12); and as David appeared before King Saul he followed such teaching to the letter.

The responsibility, then, for fanning the embers of a tired faith belongs, in part, to the Davids of this world—for along with their confidence, such men and women need to learn (perhaps to be coached in) grace, integrity and a kind of emotional intelligence if the fire in their belly is to be inspiring rather than destructive in its effects. It is not that such people should be reticent about the ways in which they have witnessed God at work: fire never spread through reticence. But grace and the ability to recognise how our words are being received remain essential attributes for those who would seek not simply to challenge a culture but to transform it—and as those called by Jesus himself to be both 'salt' and 'light' (Matthew 5:13–16), transforming the culture is the vocation of every Christian believer.

There is another responsibility, though—and that lies with the person whose faith has become tired and passionless, as they sit alone halfway up the stairs, listening to the laughter in the room next door. Self-pity can be strangely reassuring, most especially where it elicits the compassion of those around us. Cynicism can be similarly enticing, as we surround ourselves with those who feel that we're rather clever and brave to speak out as we do. Yet both are essentially self-indulgent qualities, to be practised (if at all) on unusual occasions and emphatically not to become a way of life. We can excuse Eliab, perhaps, for his sharp response to his younger brother in view of the particular pressures under which he was then labouring—in the famous words of Martin Luther, 'You can't stop birds from flying over your head'. But Eliab would also have done well to attend to the second part of that quotation: '...but you can stop them from nesting in your hair'.

In later months Saul would become anything but commendable in his attitude towards young David, but at this point in the story his conduct was exemplary. Indeed, if David unconsciously obeyed Paul's injunction to Timothy to 'set an example to the believers', Saul followed another of Paul's instructions to his young trainee, the call to 'fan into flame the gift of God, which is in you through the laying on of my hands' (2 Timothy 1:6). Back in 1 Samuel 10, Saul had been anointed with oil by the prophet Samuel, then 'set alight' by the empowering Spirit of God. Since those glory days, it had all gone horribly wrong. Yet Saul's willingness to listen to David (to ask the tough question, yes, but also to await the inspiring answer) fanned his faith into flame once more, apparently leading the king to entrust the very future of his nation to this young shepherd boy.[7] Goliath might remain an impressive bully, with armour and voice to match, but David's talk of animals on the one side and the 'living God' on the other had shifted the balance of power in Saul's heart and mind. And it's precisely that change of perspective—that ability to look at a situation through the eyes of faith — which makes the Davids of this world such a key resource for the church, and one which we ignore at our peril.

The fanatic, the cynic and the call to patient listening

The series of discussions between David, Eliab and Saul in these verses is a telling one, and at times I can identify myself with each of the protagonists, just as Henri Nouwen pictures himself in the roles of prodigal son, father and older brother in his brilliant study *The Return of the Prodigal Son*.[8] Sometimes I have been David, seeing glorious opportunities to advance the kingdom of God, and approaching vicars, bishops and even archbishops with my frequently half-baked visions and ideas. At other times I have been Eliab, paralysed and frustrated at my own lack of fruitfulness, and angered (rather than inspired) by stories of healing, transformation and church growth which seem to be taking place everywhere except for the particular stair on which I am sitting.

Yet while I pray that I will never lose the spirit of David—and while I am all too aware of the danger of allowing the spirit of Eliab to lodge in my heart—it is Saul in this passage to whom I find myself returning again and again. For as a Christian disciple, a father of four and a middle-aged church leader, the question of maintaining the fire (not forsaking my first love, in the poignant image from the risen Jesus' letter to the church in Ephesus: Revelation 2:4) is a pressing one. The best way to do it, I suspect, is to listen, and to refuse to close down that ongoing conversation with the living God himself, and to give my fullest attention to the Davids of our day, whose vision and confidence so often prove to be a beacon of hope in a confused and confusing world. A church which cold-shoulders such people will be a dying church; a church which embraces them will bear fruit thirtyfold, sixtyfold, a hundredfold (Mark 4:8).

Some years ago I was approached by a solicitor in my Notting Hill congregation, who asked whether we could meet. The church had recently completed a Mission Action Plan, following a long period of prayer and consultation, a text which set out an exciting vision for the coming five years, and I somehow assumed that this glossy new document would form the basis of our conversation. But when Tristram came to see me, he had a quite different agenda. For a while, he told me, he had had a sense that he should start a Prison Fellowship group at Wormwood Scrubs up the road—visiting the prisoners, leading Bible studies on the lifers' wing, taking part in the Sunday worship, that kind of thing. Would I maybe write him a letter of recommendation with which he could go to the prison authorities, in the hope that they might grant him access and enable him to see his vision fulfilled?

I acknowledge that my first reaction was much like that of Saul: 'You are not able to go out against this Philistine and fight him; you are little more than a boy, and he has been a warrior from his youth.' Looking at this polite, mild-mannered, young man, I couldn't imagine the kind of treatment he would receive from the 'warriors' in the lifers' wing. (I was also, I suspect, a little anxious at the possibility that our beautiful new Mission Action Plan might be knocked off course just a few days after it had rolled off the printing press!) But as Tristram spoke about his previous experience, and especially as we prayed together, the depth of his passion for the living God was both unmistakable and contagious— so much so that I duly wrote the letter and sent him off with my blessing.

Within a week Tristram had approached the prison authorities and received their permission to start a group.

Within a month he had gathered others around him (more than 20 in all) from a variety of different churches and denominations. In less than a year his team was visiting on every wing, leading three weekly Bible studies and taking part in the Sunday worship of the prison chapel. And it's true that I ended up effectively ditching our Mission Action Plan, but that was the smallest price to pay for the privilege of witnessing this latter-day David responding with such grace and confidence to the call of the living God.

— 6 —

A Right Self-Confidence: David and the Armour of Saul

'I believe that God made me for a purpose... but he also made me fast, and when I run, I feel his pleasure.'

Such are the words spoken by Eric Liddell in the film *Chariots of Fire* in an attempt to explain to his sister Jenny how running was part of his Christian calling. Whether or not the conversation actually took place is doubtful, and Jenny Liddell later objected to the film's portrayal of her as a somewhat over-pious character who tried to get Eric to concentrate less on his training and more on his missionary endeavours: 'I was a naïve, unsophisticated teenager at the time,' she wrote. 'I would never have dreamed of telling Eric what to do.'[1] Yet the questions it raises are important ones: 'Can we please God when we fully use the gifts he has given us?' and, more broadly, 'Can we discover a proper self-confidence as we freely exercise those gifts?'

In the narrative of 1 Samuel 17 we have already been introduced to one character who displayed a decidedly improper self-confidence. As we have seen, Goliath was tall, powerful, heavily armed and intimidating, self-reliant and self-assured, with one small chink in his physical armour (the absence of a visor) but no apparent chink in his psychological armour. The Philistine's confidence may have been in his brawn, not his pedigree, but with that proviso he could have echoed the words of Paul, 'If others think they have reasons to put confidence in the flesh, I have more' (Philippians 3:4). Paul's commitment to consider these natural advantages as so much 'garbage' (v. 8) for the sake of Christ, however, could not have been further removed from Goliath's bullying and self-centred agenda.

Should all self-confidence, then, be treated with suspicion from a Christian perspective? Are all our attributes just 'garbage', and our righteous deeds like 'filthy rags' (Isaiah 64:6)? There is a tendency in some Christian circles to teach that and believe it, which is part of the reason why self-confidence and arrogance have so often been equated. Yet while it is true that our salvation depends on God alone, that 'it is by grace you have been saved, through faith… not by works, so that no one can boast' (Ephesians 2:8–9), this does not in itself settle the question. Indeed, in the very next verse Paul describes us as 'God's handiwork, created in Christ Jesus to do good works'; and when we do those good works it is quite appropriate to feel God's pleasure, giving God the glory (which he deserves more than we do) but keeping for ourselves the encouragement (which we need more than he does!).

It is this sense of a godly self-confidence which comes across in the portrayal of David in 1 Samuel 17, and especially in the verses we will shortly be focusing on. David's was a confidence based on his previous experiences with lions and bears in the Bethlehem hills; a confidence which unselfconsciously spoke of his own successes and God's triumph in the same breath without fear of inconsistency; a confidence which enabled him to play to his God-given strengths, rather than submitting to expectations which would only emphasise his human weaknesses. And while it's true that David's confidence was based fair and square on the faithfulness of the living God, that did not in itself rob him of a proper *self*-confidence—for as he was later to proclaim (in an entirely different context), 'Everything comes from you, and we have given you only what comes from your hand' (1 Chronicles 29:14).

The affair of Saul's armour

> Then Saul dressed David in his own tunic. He put a coat of armour on him and a bronze helmet on his head. David fastened on his sword over the tunic and tried walking around, because he was not used to them.
>
> 'I cannot go in these,' he said to Saul, 'because I am not used to them.' So he took them off. Then he took his staff in his hand, chose five smooth stones from the stream, put them in the pouch of his shepherd's bag and, with his sling in his hand, approached the Philistine.
>
> 1 SAMUEL 17:38–40

Soldiers wear armour—and good protection and weaponry is especially critical when it comes to the fighting of duels, that novel method of settling disputes which the Philistines had introduced into the land of Canaan. Goliath wore armour, protective clothing of a most impressive kind, and here (as we have seen) he was following in the footsteps of the heroes of the Trojan War. The idea that a Menelaus or a Hector could have stepped on to the battlefield with no breastplate, sword or shield was inconceivable: indeed, the greatest possible attention was given both to the manufacture of the best armour and weaponry and to the painstaking business of putting them on and carefully adjusting them, item by item.[2]

Soldiers wear armour, and in Saul's eyes David was called to be a soldier. True, he was 'only a boy' (17:33, NIV), and would look distinctly unimpressive as he marched towards his giant opponent, but a tunic and a coat of armour, a helmet and a sword would at least give him something of the appearance of a warrior, and convey to Goliath (however weakly) that the Israelites meant business. If, by any chance, David's actions matched his rhetoric and Goliath ended up dead on the ground, the armour might serve another purpose too, providing Saul with a little of the credit for the victory, a little reflected glory. 'I didn't think it wise to offer to fight the giant myself,' Saul would have said to his men, 'but of course it was my clothing that protected the lad.' And so the king prepared to send David out as a 'model soldier', where the word 'model' is defined as a 'small imitation of the real thing'!

The sharing of armour was a normal practice in the world of *The Iliad*, even if it could prove a dangerous exercise. (Patroclus' decision to borrow the armour of his friend Achilles, for example, hastened his death as the Trojans assumed that it was Achilles they were fighting in a classic case of mistaken identity.)[3] But Saul's decision to offer David his own tunic, together with a coat of armour and a bronze helmet, was misjudged on two counts. For one thing, the height difference between the two men was substantial, with Saul described as a 'head taller than any of the [other Israelites]' (10:23) and David as 'only a boy'. Saul's tunic, then, would only trip David up and the armour weigh him down. For another, Saul was ignoring the young man's strengths and effectively playing into his weaknesses: indeed, one of the few things on which Saul, David and Eliab were all agreed was that soldiering was not part of David's expertise.

David wisely didn't accept the armour: in Robert Gordon's memorable phrase, he was not going to be 'turned into an armadillo at the drop of a helmet'.[4] His previous experience in the Bethlehem hills had revealed three considerable strengths: he was fast, full of faith and fearless. He was also, as we later discover, top of the class when it came to sling-shooting. Saul's armour would effectively constrain his mobility, compromise his faith and dampen his courage—the only gifts that the boy had to offer. And David wasn't rude or disrespectful to his king: as Saul's servant he even tried on the tunic and the armour, the helmet and the sword, although they were obviously quite unsuitable. But ultimately it was the younger man who was placing his life on the line, not the king; and whatever Saul felt, David's verdict ('I cannot go in these, because I'm not used to them') proved decisive.[5]

David stepped out not as a soldier but as a shepherd. He grasped his shepherd's staff, he took his shepherd's sling and he placed five stones in his shepherd's pouch. It was what he knew best; it was an expression of his true identity and gifting; but it was also what Israel desperately needed.

Several centuries before, as Moses was drawing to the end of his life, he had prayed, 'May the Lord, the God of the spirits of all mankind, appoint a man over this community… one who will lead them out and bring them in, so the Lord's people will not be like sheep without a shepherd' (Numbers 27:15–17, NIV)—a prayer that was immediately answered by the appointment of Joshua as Moses' successor. But now, in the valley of Elah (on the site of one of Joshua's most famous victories), a new shepherd stepped forward. To human eyes, he was only a boy, ruddy, handsome and alarmingly inexperienced. To the eye of faith, he was none other than the anointed leader of the people of God.

The 'big Yes': playing to our strengths

David's decision to reject Saul's armour would not have been possible without a clear sense of who he was and what he was called to do. In fact, the inability to say 'no', while sometimes an indication of a cheerful servant-heartedness, may on other occasions reflect a lack of clarity in our calling under God, a failure to discern the 'big Yes'[6] by which our decisions should be guided and our priorities set. The 'big Yes' in David's life—his major area of strength and expertise— was the calling to be a shepherd: in words later attributed to Asaph, one of David's worship leaders, we read, '[The Lord] chose David his servant and took him from the sheepfolds; from tending the sheep he brought him to be the shepherd of his people Jacob, of Israel his inheritance. And David shepherded them with integrity of heart; with skilful hands he led them' (Psalm 78:70–72).

Saul's attempt to clothe him as a warrior was therefore a distraction, and could (as in the case of Patroclus) have cost the younger man his life.

In the past few decades the Gallup organisation[7] has done a great deal of research on the subject of strengths—qualities they define as 'a focused combination of natural talents, skills and knowledge' which enable people to achieve 'consistent near-perfect performance' time after time. In a survey of 5000 call-centre employees, for example, they discovered that people with the same training and the same level of experience were markedly different in their effectiveness as employees. In fact, the top seven workers created 100 new loyal customers over the period of the survey, while the bottom three workers effectively lost them again!

When interviewed, the best workers seemed quite unaware of their strengths, generally assuming that what they did was 'easy' and that 'anyone could do it'. If they rang a potential customer and heard a baby crying in the background, for example, they would instinctively offer to ring back at another time, rather than pressing on regardless. At the other end of the spectrum, the workers had very little idea of what they were doing wrong, and were unhappy and demoralised. A full 800 of the employees fell into this category, regularly losing more customers than they were gaining.

It's a sobering thought that the company would have done better if it had paid for those 800 employees to stay at home and never pick up a phone again! It is still more sobering to think of other areas, church leadership among them, where the good work of some may be similarly undermined by the poor work of others.

Few people have the shepherding skills of a David or the speed of an Eric Liddell, but the sight of people playing to their God-given strengths, the 'big Yes' of their calling, can be deeply inspiring across a whole range of ministries and activities. In my last church, I can think of someone who could throw parties for 40 or 50 people, enabling each individual to feel special and included; or of someone else who instinctively seemed to get to the heart of the matter, whatever the complexity of the issues under discussion. I'm sure that neither person was aware that they were exercising the spiritual gifts of hospitality or wisdom, and both would assume (if pressed) that their gifts were very ordinary, and that anyone else could do the same. Yet the reality is that their strengths were, and are, of inestimable value to the body of Christ. Indeed, watching these people in action is the closest we come to experiencing the words attributed to St Irenaeus: 'The glory of God is a man [*sic*] fully alive.'

At this point, though, we encounter three potential difficulties, one theological, one pastoral and the third pragmatic.

On a theological level, there is a tendency among many Christians to be suspicious of the areas in which they're naturally strong, based on a misunderstanding of Paul's teaching in 2 Corinthians 12. In that chapter Paul mysteriously talks about his 'thorn in the flesh'—either a recurring sickness or disability of some kind or else a struggle with a difficult person—and tells of how he prayed three times that it might be taken from him. Instead he received an assurance from the Lord, 'My grace is sufficient for you, for my power is made perfect in weakness'; and his conclusion was entirely appropriate for one who followed a crucified Saviour: 'For when I am weak, then I am strong' (vv. 9–10).

It is true, of course, that God can use us in our weaknesses, and that the trials we go through can be purifying in their effects; it's true, too, that a strengths-based theology will become self-reliant whenever it fails to acknowledge with humility and gratitude that all things come from God. But what Paul is emphatically *not* teaching in 2 Corinthians 12 is that we should deliberately throw ourselves into Sunday school ministry if we can't stand young children or sing in the choir if we're tone deaf. Indeed it is 1 Corinthians 12, not 2 Corinthians 12, which speaks most relevantly into the issue of playing to our strengths—Paul's image of the body of Christ, where feet and hands, eyes and ears all have their part to play for the health and vitality of the whole. While some exceptional individuals may have mastered the art of walking on their hands or sketching with their feet, there's no question that life is generally easier where it's feet that do the walking and hands that do the sketching.

Having tackled the theological hurdle, the second difficulty is a pastoral one: it's all very well to praise the call-centre employees who win their company plenty of business, but what of the others who should stay at home? Gallup's research suggests that they're in the wrong job, and that no amount of additional training will reverse this conclusion. Can we claim with any degree of confidence, however, that each of those 800 has other areas of strength that are untapped in a call-centre environment—or is that just a sentimental notion with no basis in cold reality?

Both the Bible and our experience indicate that strengths are unequally shared within the human family: Jesus' parable of the talents, for example, takes it for granted that the distribution of gifts is uneven, and places its emphasis not on the number of our gifts but on the way in which we invest them (Matthew 25:14–30). Yet the image of the body of Christ—and especially Paul's insistence that 'to each one the manifestation of the Spirit is given for the common good' (1 Corinthians 12:7)—explicitly recognises that no one was absent when the gifts were handed out, that no one is dispensable; and the same assumption lies at the heart of the Gallup philosophy. Where a job or ministry role is clearly unsuited to a particular individual, it is not that that individual is useless. It is simply that they have not found the right job or ministry role.

So here we come to a third hurdle—the pragmatic question of how we go about discovering our strengths. This issue has been thoroughly covered by Rick Warren and the Gallup researchers, and I don't intend to repeat their conclusions here;[8] but one emphasis which is sometimes underplayed is the call on every Christian believer to seek out and affirm the strengths in others. The Gallup survey demonstrates that we are often slow to understand our own strengths: they come so naturally and instinctively to us that we tend to believe (quite wrongly) that they must come equally naturally and instinctively to everyone else. There is therefore a need for others to articulate our strengths for us, rather than assuming (as they often will) that we're already fully conscious of where they lie—and the same challenge applies across the Christian community.

Over the years I've rather come to dread Paul's phrase 'speaking the truth in love': in my experience as a church leader, the sentence, 'I really want to say this in love' is generally completed with the harshest of criticisms, sometimes bordering on the slanderous. But in its original context, Paul was writing about the different ministries within the church, and how each of those ministries is to be used for the building up of the body of Christ and for its steadying in the face of the winds and waves of malice and false teaching (see Ephesians 4:11–16). We can do no better service for one another, or for the body of Christ as a whole, than speaking the truth in love in this sense—articulating the strengths that we see in others, so that they might be fully released into the ministries for which God created them. Saul recognised (albeit hesitantly) that David's strengths in killing lions and bears might equip him as a giant-slayer; Jesus recognised that four fishers of fish would become key fishers of people for the kingdom of God; and thousands of years later we are still grateful for the lives of David, Peter, Andrew, James and John, and for ministries which might never have been released were it not for the discernment of a Saul or a Jesus.

Playing to our strengths is not some wooden exercise—discovering our talents, then using them again and again in a way that becomes repetitive and wearisome. (Even the best call-centre employees might do well to review their careers from time to time and assess whether their gifts could be more profitably used.) Instead there is something improvisatory about our strengths under God, a sense that we're playing as part of a jazz band rather than performing a predetermined score. A gifted trombonist in this band may take his instrument through its paces, delighting audience and fellow band members alike with the extent of his imagination and creativity. Few, perhaps, will have recognised just how beautiful the trombone can be, the heights to which it can soar, the depths to which it can plunge—yet the wise trombonist recognises both the versatility and the limitations of his instrument. True, the trombone can achieve far more than we might expect, but to seek to play it like a trumpet or a saxophone would be ridiculous.

Saying 'no': taking off Saul's armour

David knew his strengths and recognised with gratitude and humility how God had equipped him for the battle that lay ahead. His actions in these verses were therefore purposeful but improvisatory: he needed to be free to act as a shepherd—to exercise his gifts of speed, faith and courage—and not to be weighed down by the armour of Saul and the conventional expectations of those around him.

The affair of Saul's armour poses a particular challenge for us—for though it's clear that we're generally at our best, our happiest and most fruitful when we play to our strengths, it is all too easy to submit to unreasonable expectations of ourselves and our ministries, which will only trip us up or weigh us down. Such pressures may come from within or from outside: Paul, in his image of the body of Christ, addresses both scenarios (1 Corinthians 12:15, 21). Yet wherever the responsibility lies (and whatever metaphor we use), there is no question that shepherds are not at their best when they're covered with armour, that hands are not at their most effective when they're pretending to be feet, and that trombones do themselves no favours when they're masquerading as saxophones.

As someone who has specialised in the art of following gifted predecessors, I know something of the pressure to inhabit another person's 'armour'. In both Notting Hill and Twickenham—and since then too—I have been genuinely grateful for the wonderful foundations laid by some outstanding leaders, but have also felt the weight of the spiritual and emotional legacy which their ministries have left behind. Not wishing my appointment to prove a disappointment, I have tried at times to squeeze myself into the armour of these great men, often spurred on by the challenge of those who have been most indebted to their ministries—to seek to emulate the extraordinary prophetic gifts of the one and the exceptional pastoral gifts of the others. The armour in both cases has been beautifully made, an example of inspirational leadership at its very best. The only problem is that it's not been my armour. It restricts my movement, it trips me up, and I'm not used to it. And were I to remain in the armour for too long, I would eventually become paralysed, disillusioned and quite unfit for the unique role that the Lord has called on me to exercise.

Two insights have helped me shake myself free from such a debilitating condition. First (like David), I have known myself called and anointed for the job; and second (with David), I have recognised that ultimately 'the battle is the Lord's' and not mine (1 Samuel 17:47).

It's not just church expectations that can do harm to a person. Many people have been squeezed into ill-fitting armour by their parents, their peers or their partners. I recently took the funeral of a woman who'd lived with her mother almost all her life. Even when she was 73 and her mother 95, her mother would tell her when it was time to go to bed and rebuke her soundly whenever she used bad language. An extreme case, perhaps, but it's not unusual for people to go through life with the voice of a parent ringing in their ears, inadvertently encouraging them to play to their weaknesses, not to their strengths. Along with the joy of seeing people freely exercising their God-given abilities, pastoral ministry often encounters precisely the opposite: the pain of meeting people whose strengths have been buried (and lives deformed) by someone else's armour.

Jesus has something to say on this subject. To those who were weighed down by the heavy expectations of others—and especially by the teaching of the Pharisees, who as he later put it, 'tie up heavy, cumbersome loads and put them on people's shoulders, but [who] themselves are not willing to lift a finger to move them' (Matthew 23:4)—Jesus' message could not have been clearer: 'Come to me, all you who are weary and burdened, and I will give you rest' (11:28). Elsewhere he spoke not of armour but of wineskins, and pointed to the inherent impossibility of containing the new wine of the kingdom in the old wineskins of a legalism that had passed its sell-by date (9:17). It's a metaphor which works on a number of levels, but it is certainly applicable to every man or woman who has been 'born again' (John 3:3), filled with the 'wine' of the kingdom of God, and declared to be a 'new creation' (2 Corinthians 5:17).

It is not that Jesus calls us to throw off all restrictions, all commitments in the way we live. That is the message of relativism (one of the noisiest of contemporary Goliaths), not the Christian message. No, the call is rather to take off the soldier's armour so as to take up the shepherd's staff; to take off the heavy yoke of legalism so as to take on the light yoke of grace; to take off what doesn't fit because it was not custom-made for us, and to take on what fits us perfectly. 'Take my yoke upon you and learn from me, for I am gentle and humble in heart, and you will find rest for your souls. For my yoke is easy,' says Jesus (which literally means it fits well, it is custom-made), 'and my burden is light' (Matthew 11:29–30).

Towards a Christian self-confidence

In their helpful book *Self-Esteem: the Cross and Christian Confidence* (IVP, 2001), Joanna and Alister McGrath (a psychiatrist and a theologian) wrestle with the issue which lies at the heart of this chapter. It's true that their primary emphasis is on 'being' (who we are in Christ), while our focus has rather been on 'doing' (how we live confidently), but the two are closely related. In the narrative of 1 Samuel, David knows himself chosen by God, anointed by his prophet and filled with his Spirit before he goes on to confront Goliath and secure an extraordinary victory.

'Self-esteem', as the McGraths state in their introduction, 'poses a dilemma for the Christian.' On the one hand there is a desire to liberate people from a negative self-image that paralyses and distorts; on the other, there are basic tenets of the Christian gospel (such as the reality of sin, justification by grace and the call to humility) which strike at the root of secular approaches to feeling good about ourselves. 'Whoever tries to keep their life will lose it, and whoever loses their life will preserve it,' says Jesus in Luke's Gospel (17:33)—hardly a conventional starting-point for the attempt to develop a positive self-image.

It is the cross of Christ which gives us what the McGraths describe as 'the objective basis for self-esteem':

> *Where secular psychological theories close their eyes to the reality, the seriousness and the power of sin, the gospel acknowledges them—but strongly affirms the reality, the seriousness and the power of the cross of Christ to defeat sin. We may rest assured that all that is necessary for self-esteem has been done—and done extremely well!—by God through Christ on the cross. (p. 90)*

The authors fill out the implications of this cross-shaped self-esteem in terms of God's parental care, the richness of his plan of salvation and the call on his people to encourage and affirm one another; and a chapter based on Paul's letter to the Philippians helps to root these implications in normal (and contented) Christian living.

For the young shepherd boy, the full glory of God's plan had yet to be revealed—although (as Jesus himself noted) David came closer to seeing the outlines of that plan than any of his contemporaries (see Mark 12:35–37). Even without a gospel understanding of what it means to be a forgiven, reconciled child of God, however, David was able to act with confidence in the man that God had made him and the gifts that he had given him—a kind of 'creation confidence' which runs alongside the 'salvation confidence' emphasised by Joanna and Alister McGrath.

Of course, 'creation confidence' similarly needs to take account of the Fall, and of the effect of sin on our lives. It is only by the grace of God and through faith in him that our strengths can genuinely be used for his glory, for 'without faith it is impossible to please God' (Hebrews 11:6). Yet those words also imply the reverse, that *with* faith it *is* possible to please God; that the sight of young David stepping out as a shepherd, not a soldier, brought joy to the heart of his Creator. To return to the words with which we began this chapter: 'I believe that God made me for a purpose... but he also made me fast, and when I run, I feel his pleasure.'

In conclusion, perhaps the reality is this: there are times when we become cocky and self-reliant, boasting of our gifts and abilities, and it is that tendency which Jesus addresses when he instructs us, 'You also, when you have done everything you were told to do, should say, "We are unworthy servants; we have only done our duty"' (Luke 17:10). Yet there are also times when we become discouraged, lacking in confidence, paralysed by a sense that nothing we do is worth very much, that we live under the cloud of God's displeasure—and it is that state of mind which Jesus challenges in the words of the master in the parable of the talents: 'Well done, good and faithful servant! You have been faithful with a few things; I will put you in charge of many things. Come and share your Master's happiness' (Matthew 25:21).

Confidence in our Faith-Sharing: David and Goliath

At first sight it might be hard to spot the link between Hector the Trojan, Goliath the Philistine, Marshall Bruce Mathers III (more widely known to the rapping fraternity as Eminem) and Richard Dawkins the eminent biologist; but there is one attribute which connects them all. Hector had a way with words, combining a commanding physical presence with a talent for abusing his opponents: 'Ajax you've got it wrong, you great oaf... your flesh and your fat shall glut the Trojan dogs and birds of prey.'[1] Goliath had effectively learnt his trade at the school of Hector, and matched his taunting blow for blow. Eminem, rap artist and star of the movie *8 Mile*, helped to resurrect this ancient form of verbal jousting in the freestyle rap battles which feature in the film. And what of Richard Dawkins? His grammar might be a little more correct and his vocabulary wider than that of Marshall Mathers, but his description of the God of the Old Testament as a 'misogynistic, homophobic, racist, infanticidal, genocidal, filicidal, pestilential, megalomaniacal, sadomasochistic, capriciously malevolent bully'[2] almost begs for an accompanying drumbeat, and certainly belongs more to the world of the rap tournament than to the measured academic environment in which he carries out his scientific studies.

In the face of the increasingly raucous voices of a

crusading atheism, how is the church called to respond? Should Christians become raucous in return, matching the strident fundamentalism of the new atheist agenda with a strident fundamentalism of our own? Should we alternatively speak in calm and measured tones, which are at the same time entirely reasonable and deeply ineffective? Or is there a middle path, a track which boldly uses godly means to achieve godly ends, thus engendering renewed gospel confidence in ourselves and those around us? In 2 Corinthians 10, Paul writes that 'the weapons we fight with are not the weapons of the world' (v. 4), and the verse implies two things: first that as Christians we do indeed have weapons at our disposal (thus rendering the 'ineffective' option a cop-out), and second that they're of an entirely different nature from those that are used against us.

As we move towards the climax of 1 Samuel 17, we need to acknowledge once more that we are dealing with a physical battle which formed part of a long and bloody series of skirmishes between the Israelites and the Philistines. In taking this passage as a model for Christian confidence (and not, say, as part of a discussion on the theology of the 'just war') there will therefore be aspects of the story which do not apply to disciples of the Prince of Peace.[3] Yet the issue at the heart of this confrontation—David's overwhelming desire that 'the whole world [might] know that there is a God in Israel' (v. 46)—remains of the greatest possible relevance for the Christian community. Indeed, as those who are called upon to 'go and make disciples of all nations' (Matthew 28:19), it is arguable that all that we do, from the smallest act of kindness to the most extravagant display of kingdom power, should be energised and inspired by the global vision that had so gripped the heart of this young shepherd boy.

Rapping in the Valley of Elah

Meanwhile, the Philistine, with his shield-bearer in front of him, kept coming closer to David. He looked David over and saw that he was little more than a boy, glowing with health and handsome, and he despised him. He said to David, 'Am I a dog, that you come at me with sticks?' And the Philistine cursed David by his gods. 'Come here,' he said, 'and I'll give your flesh to the birds and the wild animals!'

David said to the Philistine, 'You come against me with sword and spear and javelin, but I come against you in the name of the Lord Almighty, the God of the armies of Israel, whom you have defied. This day the Lord will deliver you into my hands, and I'll strike you down and cut off your head. This very day I will give the carcasses of the Philistine army to the birds and the wild animals, and the whole world will know that there is a God in Israel. All those gathered here will know that it is not by sword or spear that the Lord saves; for the battle is the Lord's, and he will give all of you into our hands.'
1 SAMUEL 17:41–47

When David first set eyes on Goliath he was distinctly underwhelmed; and the same was true when Goliath first set eyes on David. Yet the nature of their 'underwhelming' could not have been more different. 'We live by faith, not by sight,' wrote Paul to the Corinthians (2 Corinthians 5:7), and it was this quality which distinguished the shepherd boy's reaction from that of his Philistine opponent.

For David, looking with the eyes of faith, Goliath's imposing physical presence couldn't hide the fact that he was simply an 'uncircumcised Philistine' (v. 26) with the cheek to defy the armies of the living God. For Goliath, looking with the eyes of normal sight, David's unimpressive physical presence could (and did) hide the fact that he was a shepherd of Israel, anointed and gifted by God Almighty to defend God's flock from lions, bears and giants. Within the terms of 1 Samuel itself—with its core message that 'People look at the outward appearance, but the Lord looks at the heart' (16:7)—Goliath had the perspective of the 'people', and David of 'the Lord'.

Goliath had asked for a *man* to come and fight him, and was no doubt flummoxed at the sight of an opponent who was 'little more than a boy'. We are not told the reaction of the Philistine army at this point, but we sense that they must have been somewhat wrong-footed too. It is easy to cheer on a champion when he is fighting another champion—when one tough, scarred heavyweight takes on another tough, scarred heavyweight. But what if your champion is mightily protected, heavily armed and accompanied by a shield-bearer, and his opponent is young, handsome, apparently unarmed and wearing little more than a loincloth? On the one hand it's laughable, pitiful, simply demonstrating the feebleness of an opposition which can only put forward an inexperienced boy as its champion; on the other it's uneasy, uncomfortable, with even the prospect of a straightforward victory doing little to quell the sense that the contest is hopelessly mismatched.

Goliath may have picked up some of that unease himself, but that only served to fuel his rage as he looked at David, despised him, then taunted him and cursed him by his gods. On a previous occasion the massive statue of one of those gods (Dagon) had fallen on its face before the ark of the covenant (1 Samuel 5:3), but Goliath still foolishly kept faith with an idol which had lost both its head and its hands in the incident. Meanwhile, David's wooden staff, the only

weapon that was visible to the giant, added insult to injury—
'Am I a dog, that you come at me with sticks?'—although
Goliath's use of animal imagery was particularly unfortunate
given the recent account of David's successes over lions and
bears. The giant's final salvo, while fairly standard fare at the
time,[4] was equally ill-judged: 'Come here, and I'll give your
flesh to the birds and the wild animals.' They were in every
sense Goliath's 'famous last words', and remind us perhaps
of the last words of a later military leader, General Sir John
Sedgwick, in the Battle of Spotsylvania Court House on 8
May 1864: 'They couldn't hit an elephant at this dist...'![5]

How, then, did David respond to his opponent's
psychological warfare? On one level he returned the insults
with interest, promising that he would strike Goliath down
and cut off his head before giving the carcasses of the entire
Philistine army to the birds and the wild animals: standard
fare once more. At the heart of his speech, though, was
a message that was far-reaching, fresh, visionary and
supremely confident, placing the Lord (the mighty Yahweh)
at the centre of the picture once again, and bringing the
chapter's theme of defiance to a fitting conclusion. At the
beginning of the chapter, Goliath spoke of how he defied *the
armies of Israel*' (v. 10), shouting out this challenge morning
and evening for forty days (vv. 16, 23). In response, some
of the Israelite army took Goliath's words a little further,
claiming that the giant was defying Israel as a whole and
not simply her armies (v. 25). David then raised the bar
significantly higher with his rhetorical question, 'Who is this
uncircumcised Philistine that he should defy *the armies of the
living God*?' (v. 26; see also v. 36).[6] But it was as he faced
Goliath that the full extent of the Philistine's defiance came
home to him: 'You come against me with sword and spear

and javelin, but I come against you in the name of *the Lord Almighty, the God of the armies of Israel, whom you have defied'* (v. 45).

It was the Israelites and their king who (in the face of Goliath the champion) behaved as though God were dead, and therefore needed to be reminded of the 'living God'. But it was Goliath who (in the face of David the shepherd-boy) behaved as though God were weak, and therefore needed to be reminded of the 'Lord Almighty'. And once again in David's speech we see the extent of his commitment to God's providence, an understanding which helped him to acknowledge both the Lord's role and his own in the ensuing battle. Yet the shepherd was equally sure that it was the Lord, not himself, who should be fully credited with the victory; that 'those gathered here' (both Philistines and Israelites) and indeed 'the whole world' might know that 'it is not by sword or spear that the Lord saves; for the battle is the Lord's'.

It's a perspective which the Israelites (especially their women-folk) were later to disregard. Rather than giving God the glory for the ensuing victory, a kind of cult developed around David, no doubt encouraged by his courage and his youthful good looks (see 1 Samuel 18:7). Conversely, what might sound like an empty rhetorical flourish from the mouth of David—that the 'whole world will know that there is a God in Israel'—has been fulfilled far more powerfully than anyone at the time could have imagined. The story of David and Goliath has indeed been told across the 'whole world', or at least a very large part of it, and for anyone who's taken the trouble to read it in full, the spiritual significance of this narrative is inescapable.

David's inexperience, his youthful appearance, his refusal to dress in the armour of Saul and his words to Goliath were all of a piece: they each suggested a radical dependence on Almighty God. They were also unsettling and subversive, accepting the Philistine's challenge to a duel but approaching the fight from a completely original angle. David was clear about the need for both word and action if the world were to believe that there is a God in Israel, for words without actions are ineffective, while actions without words are uninstructive. Only David's commentary (in advance of the deed itself) allows us to glimpse the true meaning of an event which might otherwise have been interpreted as a fluke, a freak accident, a testimony to David's sling-shooting abilities or a sentimental parable of the victory of the little guy over the forces that oppress him.

There's something here about a radical dependence on Almighty God, about a call to accept the challenge of our secular society but simultaneously to subvert it, about a need for both word and action if we are to share the gospel with integrity and confidence, which connects with Paul's assertion that 'the weapons we fight with are not the weapons of the world' (2 Corinthians 10:4). How, then, do we discover those weapons for ourselves? How do we commend the good news of Christ to a world where some are intrigued, many are indifferent, and an ever-increasing number are openly hostile?

The strengths and shortcomings of Christian apologetics

Throughout its history the church has produced a succession of highly articulate men and women who are gifted in the art of Christian apologetics, a systematic defence of the gospel against its pagan or secular detractors. In ancient times we think of people like the apostle Paul, Justin Martyr, Irenaeus, Tertullian, Jerome and Augustine of Hippo; in the Middle Ages, of Thomas Aquinas; and in the past hundred years, of Frances Schaeffer, C.S. Lewis, Nicky Gumbel, Alister McGrath and Amy Orr-Ewing, among many others. Each has been engaged in a vital task, which is grounded in the challenge of 1 Peter 3:15: 'Always be prepared to give an answer to everyone who asks you to give the reason for the hope that you have.'

The new atheist phenomenon has produced several responses from the apologetics stable. A number have been written by Professor Alister McGrath, whose CV includes the unusual combination of a PhD in molecular biophysics and an Oxford chair in Historical Theology. *Dawkins' God: Genes, Memes and the Meaning of Life* (Blackwell, 2005) has been followed by the briefer *The Dawkins' Delusion?: Atheistic Fundamentalism and the Denial of the Divine* (SPCK, 2007, co-authored with Joanna McGrath) and by *Why God Won't Go Away: Engaging with the New Atheists* (SPCK 2011); and the first book in particular is an example of contemporary apologetics at its best, taking the fight to Dawkins with intelligence, clarity and panache.

Christian apologetics is clearly part of the answer as we seek to communicate the gospel to the world around us—and it has the major benefit of engaging with Goliath on Goliath's own terms, of answering questions that people are genuinely asking. But there are difficulties here, too, both practical and philosophical. On a practical level, who is actually listening to the Christian apologists? And philosophically, is Christian apologetics itself a surrender to a rationalistic worldview which is already in decline?

The practical question can best be answered by some

simple statistics. *The God Delusion*, for example, has sold several million copies in the UK alone, and many millions more across the world. By comparison, the bestselling Christian apologists would do well to register sales in the tens of thousands, figures suggestive of an audience which is largely Christian anyway.

In a previous generation, C.S. Lewis' books had mass appeal, reaching out to people who had lived through at least one and even two World Wars, and reassuring them that they could still hold on to the historic faith without committing intellectual suicide. In today's world, though, it is becoming more and more difficult to communicate a defence of the gospel beyond the boundaries or, at best, the fringes of the church community. That doesn't invalidate the exercise, of course: David's passion was for 'all those gathered here', both Israelites and Philistines, and restoring the church's confidence in the living God and the truth of the gospel is a most important task. But the reality is that few of today's 'Philistines' (in my analogy) will take the time and trouble to look at both sides of the argument, and that we live in an age when competent God-bashing books will generally outsell competent God-embracing books by 100 to one.

The philosophical question is equally pressing, and is well expressed in the clash of cultures between David the Hebrew and Goliath the Greek. David's willingness to engage with Goliath, and to do so in the Greek-inspired form of a duel, has already been noted; but so has the fact that his approach was essentially subversive, responding to his Philistine opponent from an entirely original angle. David didn't match might with might, weapon with weapon, armour with armour. Instead he balanced Goliath's advantages on the one hand (his sword and spear and javelin) with the name of the

Lord on the other, in a way that clearly favoured the name of the Lord.

The danger of a Christian apologetics, which (since the days of Thomas Aquinas at least) has largely assumed that the rationalist world of the Greeks is the ground on which the battle should be fought, is that it can end up short-changing the gospel, a life-changing message which, as Paul himself concedes, is 'foolishness' to the Greeks (see 1 Corinthians 1:23). In many respects, Christian believers approach life from a radically different starting-point than their secular counterparts: indeed, the belief system that underlies the secular worldview is itself open to serious criticism. Yet the practice of Christian apologetics can too easily concede the basis on which the debate is to be decided, and use much the same armour and weaponry as its secular opponents.

Lesslie Newbigin writes brilliantly on this theme in *Proper Confidence*. 'The reasonableness of Christianity', as he puts it, 'will be demonstrated... not by adjusting its claims to the requirements of a pre-existing structure of thought but by showing how it can provide an alternative foundation for a different structure' (p. 93). Newbigin is scathing about a theological liberalism which has largely tried to constrict the new wine of the gospel in the old wineskins of Greek rationalism (my image, not his); but he is equally critical of a fundamentalism which replaces the lively Hebrew notion of biblical inspiration with the dreary Greek notion of biblical inerrancy. If our faith is primarily based on reason, it will never lead us to the living God, let alone the cross of Christ. If our faith is primarily based on the inerrancy of every passing scriptural reference, it will focus in the wrong direction and all too easily lead to a 'kind of hard rationalism that is remote from grace'. 'The gospel is not a matter of indubitable certainties,' Newbigin concludes: 'it is the offer of a grace that can only be accepted in faith, a faith in which both heart and intellect join' (pp. 99–100).

If contemporary Christian apologetics at its best is only part of the answer to the philosophical Goliaths of our age, we need to discover the rest of that answer: an approach to proclaiming and living out our faith which is proactive not reactive, confident not embarrassed, on the front foot and not on the defensive. The three features that we have already noted in David's approach—his radical dependence on God, his ability simultaneously to accept Goliath's challenge and to subvert it, and his commitment to word and action—will each play a part in this confident proclamation. And it's in our reading of the Bible itself, and the writings of the earliest Christian apologists, that we discover resources for this task which are deeply rooted in the faith of the shepherd boy, yet remain hugely relevant for the mission of the church three thousand years on.

'Not by Sword or Spear'

David's vision that 'all those gathered here will know that it is not by sword or spear that the Lord saves' encompassed both Israelites and Philistines: in fact, the same gospel confidence which inspires those within the church will generally inspire those outside it, too. The early chapters of the book of Acts present us with a supremely confident church, living out the life of the kingdom with generosity, prayerfulness and gospel power. It is hardly surprising in such a context that 'the Lord added to their number daily those who were being saved' (2:47).

In his second letter to the Corinthians, Paul commended

his gospel ministry to his Christian readership—and his words could equally be taken as a justification of his ministry to the wider world. He wrote:

As servants of God we commend ourselves in every way: in great endurance; in troubles, hardships and distresses; in beatings, imprisonments and riots; in hard work, sleepless nights and hunger; in purity, understanding, patience and kindness; in the Holy Spirit and in sincere love; in truthful speech and in the power of God; with weapons of righteousness in the right hand and in the left; through glory and dishonour, bad report and good report; genuine, yet regarded as impostors; known, yet regarded as unknown; dying, and yet we live on; beaten, and yet not killed; sorrowful, yet always rejoicing; poor, yet making many rich; having nothing, and yet possessing everything. (6:4–10)

It's a powerful outburst, exposing both Paul's heart and his demanding apostolic experience to his Corinthian readers. But it also contains references to at least five key weapons at the Christian's disposal, weapons which are not of this world, but which effectively combine both word and action.

The first and most costly weapon consists of the Christians' willingness to embrace suffering: their courage, even joy, amid 'troubles, hardships and distresses... hard work, sleepless nights and hunger', as Paul put it. The earliest apologists took up this theme, especially in the context of persecution. In the words of the second-century epistle to Diognetus:

Have you not seen Christians flung to the wild beasts to make them deny their Lord, and yet remain undefeated? Do you not see how the more of them suffer such punishments, the larger grows the number of the rest? These things do not look like the work of man; they are the power of God, and the evident tokens of his presence.[7]

The account of the martyrdom of Polycarp (c. AD69–155), the elderly Bishop of Smyrna, also remains one of the most poignant narratives in ancient literature.

'We also glory in our sufferings,' writes Paul, 'because we know that suffering produces perseverance; perseverance, character; and character, hope' (Romans 5:3–4); and whether through persecution or suffering of other kinds, the impact of a courageous Christian can be truly remarkable, bringing credibility to the gospel message in a way that mere words will never do. As a hospice manager wrote of a much-loved member of my then congregation, who eventually died following a three-year battle with cancer, 'Her time in Michael Sobell House completely changed the outlook of many people who worked there: many people came into her room and left inspired.'

The second weapon in the Christian's armoury consists of the miraculous power of the Spirit to bring revelation, healing and freedom—God's people commending themselves and their Lord 'in the Holy Spirit... and in the power of God', as Paul put it. In Chapter 4 we considered the remarkable rise of the Pentecostal movement, with its emphasis on both the word of God and the miraculous works of God, and this is a strong theme in the ministry of Jesus and of the early church. Augustine of Hippo (354–430), for example, was initially sceptical about the continuing availability of the power to heal, but he later changed his mind. As he records in *The City of God*:

I realised how many miracles were occurring in my own day, and how wrong it would be to allow the memory of these marvels

to perish from among our people. It is only two years ago that
the keeping of records was begun here in Hippo, and already we
have nearly seventy attested miracles.[8]

Part of the ongoing fruitfulness of the Alpha Course[9] lies in its
openness to this spiritual dynamic alongside its engagement
with standard apologetics questions such as 'Who was Jesus?'
and 'Why did Jesus die?' While the academic discussion
rages, it's often difficult to see what progress is being made,
but when someone is healed, or filled with God's Spirit, or
sees their prayers positively (even dramatically) answered, it
is hard to ignore the sense that the living God is somehow at
work even as his very existence is being vigorously contested.
The task of the course leaders changes from that moment on:
like Peter and John at the Beautiful Gate (Acts 3), their job is
both to challenge any wrong interpretation of what has just
happened ('Why do you stare at us as if by our own power
or godliness we had made this man walk?' v. 12) and to
proclaim the right interpretation of what has just happened
('It is Jesus' name and the faith that comes through him that
has given this complete healing to him, as you can all see',
v. 16, NIV); and from that moment on, in Jesus' memorable
phrase, the fields are 'ripe for harvest' (John 4:35).

The third weapon is that of a simple, heartfelt sharing
of the gospel treasure through words and a transformed
life—'poor, yet making many rich; having nothing and
yet possessing everything', as Paul puts it, recalling Jesus'
parable of the man who sold everything to buy a field
in which treasure lay (Matthew 13:44). This preaching
of the gospel was, of course, Paul's primary calling, and
he was unashamed of its content, since he himself had
experienced Christ as 'the power of God and the wisdom of

God' (1 Corinthians 1:24). On two occasions in the book of Acts[10] we see Paul using that road-to-Damascus experience to explain the transformation in his understanding and character; and personal testimony continued to play a part in evangelism in the next generations too, demonstrating that the gospel was not simply a matter of words but of transforming power.

There is a famous passage in the first Apology of Justin Martyr (100–165) where he writes:

> *We who formerly delighted in fornication now embrace chastity alone… we who valued above all things the acquisition of wealth and possessions now bring all that we have into a common stock and share it out according to their need; we who hated and destroyed one another… now pray for our enemies and endeavour to persuade those who hate us unjustly to conform their lives to the good precepts of Christ.*[11]

It is not difficult to imagine Justin preaching this message to his pagan contemporaries, some of whom, at least, aspired to the kind of values that the Christians lived by. I heard a similar message delivered by a member of my former congregation, who discovered in Christ the power to break free from decades of alcoholism. For the desire for personal transformation remains an important quest for many in our own day, which is why Christian testimony (both ordinary and sensational) can be such a powerful evangelistic tool.

'By this everyone will know that you are my disciples, if you love one another,' taught Jesus in John 13:35, and the fourth weapon at the Christian's disposal lies in the power of Christian loving, both within and outside the fellowship: the 'patience, kindness and… sincere love' which Paul refers to in his defence before his Corinthian detractors.

At times the early church found this area as much of a struggle as we do—in the words of Michael Green, 'Greed and arrogance threatened the fellowship in Corinth, disunity in Philippi and Rome, immorality in the churches to which 2 Peter and Jude were directed, and snobbery among the recipients of James.'[12] Perhaps such problems were inevitable in the unique experiment that brought together male and female, Jew and Gentile, slave and slave-owner on the same terms and around the same table. Yet the speed with which these difficulties were dealt with is proof of the Christians' conviction that loving fellowship was fundamental to the spread of the gospel; and Tertullian's description of the *agape* love which characterised the Christian community of his day is particularly striking, especially the practical care given:

> *... to supply the wants of boys and girls who are destitute of means and parents, and of old people now confined to the house, and such as have suffered shipwreck... or any who happen to be in the mines or banished to the islands or shut up in prison for their fidelity to God's Church.*[13]

It's no wonder that the North African church experienced a remarkable revival at the time, as the *koinonia* within the Christian congregations proved far richer and more rewarding than that of the pagan clubs (*collegia*) and taverns (*thermopolia*).

Loving fellowship—together with the loving commitment to justice which has inspired some of the most charismatic and influential Christian leaders of the past two centuries and more[14]—still has an almost unique power to draw people to Christ and to commend the gospel to a cynical world. During the Soul in the City mission in 2004, where over 20,000 teenagers descended on London to share the love of Christ, it was moving to witness both the fellowship in the campsites (where the young people ate, slept and worshipped) and the activity in the housing estates (where they threw themselves into cleaning, painting, graffiti-clearance and the running of children's clubs). On our local Ivybridge estate, the sight of these young people serving the community made a massive impact—so much so that we started a new church off the back of it; and the same will always be true when the love within the Christian community spills out on to the streets, bringing hope, justice, compassion and encouragement in its wake.

The fifth and final weapon is what Paul describes as 'truthful speech', for the power of Christian truth, when relevantly explained and expounded, is quite remarkable, with those of every generation sharing in the experience of the disciples on the road to Emmaus: 'Were not our hearts burning within us while he talked with us on the road and opened the Scriptures to us?' (Luke 24:32). The early apologists were committed to this, with Paul renting a lecture hall in Ephesus for daily discussions (see Acts 19:9) and Origen (from his teenage years upwards) leading a school 'for elementary instruction in the faith';[15] and the account we are given of the conversion of Gregory demonstrates Origen's teaching skill at its best. As Gregory later put it,

He possessed a rare combination of a certain sweet grace and persuasiveness, along with a strange power and constraint... It felt like having the warmth of the true Sun begin to rise upon us. It felt like being pierced by Origen's words as by an arrow.[16]

In those early days (as today) it was impossible to pretend that Christian truth was easily compatible with the truth claims that surrounded it. The Greek word *logos*, for example, was familiar across the Mediterranean as the ultimate impersonal entity which held the cosmos together; yet the moment John wrote that the *logos* had become flesh and lived among us as a man (let alone a man who had reportedly been executed as a criminal), most of his readers must have closed his book and written it off as nonsense. That didn't mean, however, that the Christian faith was incoherent; it simply meant that it began from a radically original starting point, from the incarnation, life, death and resurrection of Jesus of Nazareth. And the best of the early apologists and teachers were able to demonstrate how that starting point made better sense of the universe and of life as we experience it than that of its Jewish, pagan and rationalist alternatives. It also, by and large, made for better people.

Taking that approach to our contemporary situation, we need to ask whether the new atheists' starting point (that natural selection explains almost everything) is the right one, and whether we subscribe, say, to Richard Dawkins' argument that religion originated through so-called 'memes', a kind of cultural virus whose existence is entirely unproven. Is goodness simply a thinly disguised means of personal or genetic survival? Is love just a 'misfiring instinct', an accidental by-product of evolution? Is Dawkins' vision of a warm and compassionate atheistic world very plausible, when the only evidence we have to go on is so very unpromising (Stalin's Soviet Union, Pol Pot's Cambodia, Mao's China and the state of North Korea today)? The extraordinary popularity of *The God Delusion* was no doubt stoked by the appalling events of 9/11, but we shouldn't underestimate the importance of coherent, relevant, biblical teaching to provide an alternative worldview both to militant Islam and to the new atheists.

Now is a time for confidence in our teaching and preaching, rather than embattled defensiveness.

The building up of Christ's body

The willingness to embrace suffering, the miraculous work of the Spirit, the heartfelt sharing of gospel treasure, the power of Christian loving, the commitment to truthful speech—in selecting these five weapons at the Christian's disposal, I am not making some bogus allegorical link with the five smooth stones of 1 Samuel 17! But I do have in my mind another 'five' in scripture—the fivefold ministry of the church in Ephesians 4:11–13:

So Christ himself gave the apostles, the prophets, the evangelists, the pastors and teachers, to equip his people for works of service, so that the body of Christ may be built up until we all reach unity in the faith and in the knowledge of the Son of God and become mature, attaining to the whole measure of the fullness of Christ.

Apostles (as Paul demonstrates conclusively in his Corinthian correspondence) are especially called to embrace suffering: 'It seems to me that God has put us apostles on display at the end of the procession, like those condemned to die in the arena. We have been made a spectacle to the whole universe, to angels as well as to human beings' (1 Corinthians 4:9). Prophets are called to speak and move in the power of the living God. Evangelists are called to preach good news through transformed lives and transforming words; pastors and teachers to continue the ministry of the One who is 'full of grace and truth' (John 1:14).

Words are not enough in any of these ministries, but nor

are uninterpreted actions: 'How can they believe in the one of whom they have not heard? And how can they hear without someone preaching to them?' as Paul succinctly put it in Romans 10:14. What is needed is rather a radical dependence on Almighty God, an ability simultaneously to accept the challenge of our detractors and to subvert it through behaviour that is grace-filled and unexpected, together with a powerful harnessing of both word and action to equip God's people, to build up his church and to enable the 'whole world' to know that 'there is a God in Israel'.

— 8 —

Confidence-Imparting Leadership:
Two Gods, Two Destinies

Darwin E. Smith is hardly a household name, even to avid readers of the *Financial Times* and *Wall Street Journal*, but from 1971 to 1991 he turned around the fortunes of Kimberly-Clark, a poorly performing paper company, in one of the great corporate success stories of the 20th century. Smith was formerly a somewhat awkward in-house lawyer, who chose just a single word to describe his leadership style, the term 'eccentric'. He wore ill-fitting clothes, kept firmly out of the limelight and never cultivated hero status. 'He found his favourite companionship among plumbers and electricians,' writes Jim Collins, 'and spent his vacations rumbling around his Wisconsin farm… digging holes and moving rocks.'[1]

The fact that few have heard of Darwin E. Smith is no coincidence, for in his research into eleven US companies whose performance moved from 'good to great', Jim Collins discovered that all eleven were led by similarly unflamboyant characters. Such a finding was a surprise, not least to Collins himself. In a celebrity culture it is easy to assume that the best leaders will be those with a high profile, a charismatic personality and the ability to scintillate in front of shareholders and cameramen. Yet Collins' research demonstrated that these extravert character traits, while sometimes helpful to a company in the short term, could be seriously damaging over the long haul. The attempt to build a celebrity reputation proved incompatible with the commitment to build a seriously successful company.

What, then, were the shared characteristics of these eleven 'good to great' leaders? Collins summarised them in two phrases: an 'extreme personal humility' combined with an 'intense professional will'. Humility was expressed in the leaders' tendency to deflect praise away from themselves while accepting personal responsibility for corporate mistakes and failings: in interview their conversation was peppered with comments like 'I hope I'm not sounding like a big shot' or 'If the board hadn't picked such great successors, you probably wouldn't be talking with me today.' Professional will was demonstrated in a dogged commitment to see the company succeed both through big (and frequently bold) decisions and through a 'personal style of sheer workmanlike diligence'. One of the eleven compared his leadership approach to that of another (less successful) CEO: 'He was more of a show horse, whereas I was more of a plough horse.'[2]

'Level 5' leaders (as Collins went on to describe them)[3] are more concerned about the prosperity and long-term viability of the company than about their own prosperity and long-term viability. They are happy to surround themselves with gifted individuals, rather than regarding such people as a liability or a threat. They are living embodiments of U.S. President Harry Truman's dictum, 'You can accomplish anything in life, provided that you do not mind who gets the credit.' They work hard to ensure the success of their successors, rather than setting them up to fail.

And Level 5 leadership is not confined to the rarefied world of Wall Street and the Stock Exchange, nor indeed to the leadership of nations, where Mahatma Gandhi and Nelson

Mandela particularly stand out as men of extreme personal humility and intense professional will.[4] It is daily lived out in schools, communities, churches, hospitals and families, releasing confidence and enabling teams to move from good to great through the modesty and dogged determination of their leaders. I have been privileged to know a number of such people myself, from extraordinary mothers through to inspirational teachers by way of fruitful clergy and diligently hardworking Members of Parliament. Their names may well not appear in many history books, but their achievements will often prove far more significant than those of many of their higher-profile contemporaries.

Was David a 'Level 5' leader? At first sight, we might think not. Young, attractive, profoundly charismatic in both a theological and secular sense, David stepped into the limelight in the Valley of Elah and barely left it thereafter. His older brother's accusation that David was wicked and conceited may have been unfair, but there is no sense in which the young shepherd appeared publicity-shy. Here, unquestionably, was a man of passion and determination, with a brilliant career ahead of him; but whether he had the requisite humility to transform Israel itself, to build a great and confident nation, was far less clear. Even David's motivation in the first part of the chapter, combining visionary talk of the 'armies of the living God' with mercenary talk of rewards and tax breaks, sent out a distinctly mixed message. David, we might conclude, was more a charismatic Level 4 leader than a man summoned to the heights of Level 5.

Yet first impressions can be deceptive. As we move into the account of the actual fight, there are signs that David was a bigger man than we might have suspected, a leader with the potential (however raw and unformed) to turn Israel itself from good to great. Nine chapters back, the Israelites had asked Samuel for a king so that they might be 'like all the other nations, with a king to lead us and to go out before us and fight our battles' (8:20). Now, for the first time, we have a hint of how that theologically ambiguous request might be successfully met without usurping the kingship of God or compromising the vocation of his people to serve as a 'kingdom of priests and a holy nation' (Exodus 19:6).

The battle

As the Philistine moved closer to attack him, David ran quickly towards the battle line to meet him. Reaching into his bag and taking out a stone, he slung it and struck the Philistine on the forehead. The stone sank into his forehead, and he fell face down on the ground.

So David triumphed over the Philistine with a sling and a stone; without a sword in his hand he struck down the Philistine and killed him.

David ran and stood over him. He took hold of the Philistine's sword and drew it from the sheath. After he killed him, he cut off his head with the sword.

When the Philistines saw that their hero was dead, they turned and ran. Then the men of Israel and Judah surged forward with a shout and pursued the Philistines to the entrance of Gath and to the gates of Ekron. Their dead were strewn along the Shaaraim road to Gath and Ekron. When the Israelites returned from chasing the Philistines, they plundered their camp.

David took the Philistine's head and brought it to Jerusalem; he put the Philistine's weapons in his own tent.

1 SAMUEL 17:48–54

The fight, as predicted, was a hopeless mismatch. After a magnificent 47-verse build-up, the encounter itself was over almost before it began. What was not predicted (except by the shepherd-boy himself) was the outcome of the battle, a turn of events which so wrong-footed the Philistine army that it completely fell apart. Logically there were two constructive options open to the soldiers: either to throw themselves onto the mercy of Saul (in accordance with Goliath's terms in verse 9), or else to ignore the terms and take the battle to the Israelites. The fact that they chose a third option, one which would leave their bodies strewn along the road to Gath and Ekron, was a clear indication that the Philistines were simply not thinking straight.

During his discussions with King Saul, David had used a series of short, sharp verbs to describe his encounters with lions and bears: 'went, struck, rescued, seized, struck [again], killed' (v. 35). Now the narrator does the same as he reports David's encounter with Goliath: 'ran, slung, struck, struck [again], killed' (vv. 48–50). It's all very vivid, very fast-moving, and again, it invites comparison with *The Iliad*, where much space is given to speeches and to preparations for the fight, but where, as E.V. Rieu observed, 'Death... nearly always comes quickly and cleanly after a single blow'.[5]

While David's victory over Goliath was a remarkable event which strongly suggested that 'there is a God in Israel', it was not strictly a miracle. In the book of Judges we are introduced to one of the most powerful resources in the army of the tribe of Benjamin: alongside 26,000 swordsmen we read of 700 soldiers who were left-handed, 'each of whom could sling a stone at a hair and not miss' (20:16).[6] And when we consider that a sling (in the hands of a skilful soldier) held stones the size of cricket balls which could be propelled at a speed of up to 100 miles per hour, it's clear that we're talking serious weaponry here. David did not command Goliath to topple over in the name of the living God. Instead David picked the one spot where his opponent was vulnerable and hit it with unerring accuracy.

Did the stone kill Goliath or merely stun him? The text suggests that it probably did the full job, with Goliath's subsequent decapitation merely adding to the joy and elation of the Israelites and the confusion and panic of their Philistine opponents.[7] Goliath's weapons were taken to David's tent. His sword was later moved from there and ended up in the sanctuary at Nob, where David claimed it once again during his flight from King Saul (1 Samuel 21:9).[8] Goliath's head, we're told, was brought to Jerusalem—although this can only have happened after the city was captured from the Jebusites in 2 Samuel 5. There is even an intriguing piece of speculation that the word 'Golgotha', the so-called 'Place of the Skull' at which Jesus was crucified, was derived from the word 'Goliath', and may have been the name of a particular rock formation, or even the place where the giant's head was thought to be buried.[9]

For a time, David disappears from the story. As he quietly picked up his enemy's weapons and carried them off to his tent, it was left to the 'men of Judah and Israel' to chase the Philistines back to their cities of Gath and Ekron, with a series of action words of their own: 'surged, pursued, chased, plundered' (vv. 52–53). No attempt was made to sack those cities (or the neighbouring Philistine towns of Ashkelon, Gaza and Ashdod): the emphasis here was on a defence of Israel's territory rather than the destruction of all things Philistine. But it was still a bloody affair as the Israelites broke free from their 40 days of paralysis and took the fullest advantage of that freedom; and the account of the bloodshed and the subsequent plundering of the Philistine camp is presented to us with neither ethical nor editorial comment.

Perhaps the most significant observation is that David didn't lead the charge. Having secured such a spectacular victory over Goliath, he might have been expected to press ahead, the Israelites right behind him, killing his tens of thousands as he was later reputed to have done (18:7). But that was not the job entrusted to him by Saul: that was the job of the 'men of Judah and Israel' (David's brothers among them) under the leadership of the king's officers. It was not simply David, in other words, who ended that day with an extraordinary story to tell his children and grandchildren in the years to come. It was thousands of ordinary people— Saul's men from both the southern tribes of Judah and the northern tribes of Israel—who would each have their personal account of the triumph, and how they'd played their part in the defeat of the Philistines on that momentous day.

David's ability to withdraw to his tent at this point, to appear graciously and humbly before the king and to allow the troops and officers to share in the victory, sends out a powerful message, the message of the Level 5 leader—that both determination and humility are key to genuine success, the success that releases confidence in a team (or church, army or nation) rather than focusing that confidence around a single charismatic individual. We stand in awe of Level 4 leadership and its extraordinary range of gifts and talents; but the Level 5 leader makes us rather stand in awe of ourselves, or (at the very least) leaves us surprised at the abilities with which God has entrusted us—qualities which will often remain submerged until the right kind of leadership helps to draw them out.

Later in David's life we read of how he surrounded himself with champions: the so-called Three who all had extraordinary achievements to their name, and the Thirty who were also honoured for their courage (2 Samuel 23)[10]—a far cry from the days of King Saul, who couldn't find *one* of his fighting men prepared to take on the Philistine giant. Later still, we read of how David set up his successor to succeed: instead of sulking at the news that Solomon, rather than himself, was being called to build the Jerusalem temple, David went about raising the money and the workforce for this huge enterprise, so that his son would have all that he needed to get going the moment he ascended to the throne (1 Chronicles 22). And one of the most moving indications of David's Level 5 credentials occurred just a few days before his death, when a group of royal officials came to his bedside with the words, 'May your God make Solomon's name more famous than yours and his throne greater than yours' (1 Kings 1:47a). A lesser leader (of the Level 4 variety) would have choked at such a sentiment, or demanded that the officials be dismissed or worse; but David, we're told, humbly 'bowed in worship on his bed and said, "Praise be to the Lord, the God of Israel, who has allowed my eyes to see a successor on my throne today"' (vv. 47b–48).

Humility and fierce determination; the ability to place the prosperity and long-term viability of the company (or, in David's terms, the nation) above the leader's own prosperity and long-term viability; the calling to be a plough horse rather than a show horse; the commitment to the building up of others (both colleagues and successors) rather than to the massaging of the leader's ego: there is something in this combination of qualities which suggests that David—and more especially Jesus of Nazareth, the 'Son of David'—might be able to teach us a thing or two about Level 5 leadership.

Leadership lessons in the valley and the wilderness

David's entry on the scene in 1 Samuel 16—17 has some clear parallels with Jesus' first appearance in the Gospels of Matthew, Mark and Luke. It's not that we are given any Davidic birth narrative to rival those in the first or third Gospels (or, indeed, the story of Samuel's birth in 1 Samuel 1:1—2:11). But the account of the young shepherd's anointing as king in the presence of his brothers is strongly echoed in the story of Jesus' baptism, with Samuel and John the Baptist playing much the same role as both prophets and kingmakers.

Samuel used oil, while John used water, but both materials were merely outward and visible signs of the anointing of God's Spirit who 'came on David in power' (1 Samuel 16:13) and descended on Jesus 'like a dove' (Mark 1:10). From the outset of their ministries, both David and Jesus would be dependent on the Spirit, yet their callings would prove to be very different. David (on whom the Spirit came in power) would 'shed much blood' and '[fight] many wars' on his way to building a strong and united nation, something that would disqualify him from the holy task of building God's temple (1 Chronicles 22:8–9). Jesus (on whom the Spirit came like a dove) would be known as the 'Prince of Peace', called to a ministry of compassion, healing and reconciliation: a 'shepherd' like his ancestor, but also the Passover lamb who would 'give his life as a ransom for many' (Mark 10:45).

Yet after baptism comes testing; after anointing comes conflict. David, as we've seen, was sent by his father Jesse to the Valley of Elah, where he was called to face a formidable human opponent who for 40 mornings and evenings had been terrorising the people of God; Jesus was sent by the Spirit of his heavenly Father to the Judean wilderness, where he was called to face a formidable spiritual opponent who tested him for 40 days and nights during a time of fasting, prayer and intense spiritual struggle. Both Goliath and the devil did a great line in bullying provocation, and both David and Jesus responded with references to the God of the exodus story: the 'living God' on the lips of David, the 'Lord your God' on the lips of Jesus.[11]

1 Samuel 17 and Mark 1:12–13[12] are presented in the form of a duel, with one man pitted against a powerful opponent. But in each case the hero of the story was more than a private individual—he was also a representative of the nation as a whole. David's victory over Goliath was final and decisive; Jesus' victory over the devil—at this point, at least—was partial and temporary. Yet Mark's account (which alone mentions that Jesus was 'with the wild animals', 1:13), may suggest that this battle was more akin to David's private skirmishes with lions and bears than to the public victory in the Valley of Elah. The decisive triumph was still to come, as each of the Gospels move inexorably from baptism and temptation through to cross and resurrection.

There is a parallel, too, in the aftermath of the battle, for while David immediately called the men of Judah and Israel to press home the advantage, Jesus directly summoned his first disciples, representatives of the twelve tribes of Israel,[13] to do the same. When he later sent them out (along with

60 others) to preach the gospel and heal the sick, he was thrilled by their excited testimony, 'Lord, even the demons submit to us in your name' (Luke 10:17), and—in a visionary moment—saw Satan dethroned, toppled from a place of real power and authority. In the terms of 1 Samuel 17, it's as though the 72 had surged forward with a victory shout, pursuing the demons back to where they came from, pushing forward the boundaries of the kingdom of light and reasserting the truth that 'the earth is the Lord's, and everything in it' (Psalm 24:1).

Yet perhaps the most telling connection between David and Jesus lies in the sense that both men were here flexing their leadership muscles and testing out the kind of ministry they would be called upon to exercise. We have seen how David was a little too interested in the potential rewards that would come his way through taking on his mighty opponent, but that he also demonstrated humility and good judgement near the end of the story. Jesus was similarly tempted by the trappings of power—by a style of leadership that was arrogant, showy, self-serving and dictatorial (see Matthew 4:3–9), yet he consistently rejected the devil's advances and embraced instead the servant leadership reflected in the great hymn of Philippians 2, culminating in his obedience to death, 'even death on a cross' (v. 8).

Perhaps it was during those 40 days in the wilderness that Jesus became the archetypal Level 5 leader.

Trying and training

For those of us charged with the task of leading a team (from the smallest family unit to the largest multinational corporation), these reflections on David and Jesus leave one crucial question unanswered: is Level 5 attainable by the many or only by the few? Jim Collins suggests that there are two categories of people here: a smaller group who 'could never in a million years bring themselves to subjugate their egotistic needs to the greater ambition of building something larger and longer-lasting than themselves', and a larger group who 'under the right circumstances… have the potential to evolve to Level 5'. Certain events, he continues, might provide the catalyst for such a potential to be realised—perhaps a period of self-reflection, a significant life experience, the adoption of a wise mentor or a religious conversion. But there will always be some, he contends, who simply 'do not have the seed of Level 5' within them.

As Christians, we cannot be content with so fatalistic a prognosis. It's not that everyone is called to be a Nelson Mandela or a Darwin E. Smith, let alone a David or a Jesus, but the idea that it is impossible for an individual to grow in the basic values of humility, determination and a vision larger than themselves is incompatible with the key Judeo-Christian doctrines of the image of God and the transforming work of his Spirit. When Paul wrote that Jesus, 'being in very nature God' took 'the very nature of a servant' (Philippians 2:6–7), he was not suggesting that *despite* the fact that Jesus was God, he came to serve (as in the old Greek myths where Zeus and Hermes came down to earth dressed as slaves, then threw off their rags to reveal themselves in all their Olympian splendour). He was rather asserting that *because of* the fact that he was God, Jesus came to serve—that Jesus' servant role revealed, not disguised, the God who is Love. And if men and women are made in the image of this God, and are open to the power of his Spirit, there is no reason why even the most self-centred of individuals should lack the potential to be transformed into the most modest and visionary of Level 5 leaders.

The New Testament is full of Level 5 admonitions. Even the three chapters that comprise the Sermon on the Mount have quite enough for the would-be leader to reflect on: 'Blessed are the meek, for they will inherit the earth' (Matthew 5:5); 'When you give to the needy, do not announce it with trumpets, as the hypocrites do... to be honoured by others' (6:2); 'Do not store up for yourselves treasures on earth' (6:19); 'Take the plank out of your own eye, and then you will see clearly to remove the speck from the other person's eye' (7:5); 'In everything, do to others what you would have them do to you' (7:12). There is no trace of the egotist here, but nor is there any suggestion that Jesus is merely addressing those with an inherent capacity to behave in this way. All are created in the image of God (Genesis 1:27); 'all have sinned and fall short of the glory of God' (Romans 3:23); 'God our Saviour... wants all people to be saved and to come to a knowledge of the truth' (1 Timothy 2:3–4). Creation and the fall are universal, in other words, and so is the potential scope of the salvation that frees us from our bondage to pride and self-centredness and enables us to live as children of God.

Mention of the fall suggests that the cultivation of Level 5 qualities is not a straightforward exercise—that for many people (at least) there is a natural self-absorption which militates against an 'extreme personal humility', and a latent lethargy which threatens to swamp an 'intense professional will'. Jim Collins, as we've seen, suggests how these tendencies might be counteracted through a period of reflection, a significant life experience, a wise mentor and so on, and he also encourages his readers to practise the other principles in his book—in effect, to try harder. But in the stories of David in the valley and Jesus in the wilderness we have significantly deeper resources to draw on—the anointing of God's Holy Spirit on the one hand, and the practice of the spiritual disciplines on the other.

Both David and Jesus stepped on to the battlefield as those anointed with the Spirit of God, as expressed through the sacramental elements of oil and water and initiated through the human agency of Samuel and John the Baptist. They were therefore acting in the power of the Spirit, and humbly acknowledging that 'the battle is the Lord's' (1 Samuel 17:47), a Lord who alone should be followed, served and worshipped (see Matthew 4:10). 'Come, Holy Spirit' is an ancient prayer which has recently been revived in both catholic and charismatic circles, and every Christian believer (especially those called to Christ-like leadership) should pray such a prayer both regularly and fervently. The encouragement of being prayed for by the Samuels and John the Baptists of our day (those who will stand alongside us and bless us) should also be a normal part of our Christian living, as should the sacramental use of water and oil—and, of course, of bread and wine—through which Christ renews, anoints and nourishes us in his service.

Both David and Jesus stepped on to the battlefield as those practised in the spiritual disciplines, too: David as a mighty worshipper, 'Israel's singer of songs' (2 Samuel 23:1, NIV), Jesus as a man deeply nourished through the scriptures and remarkably capable of maintaining a 40-day fast. Being filled with the Spirit does not, in other words, negate the need for spiritual discipline; indeed the two go hand in hand. And while this is not the place for a detailed exposition of the subject, the insights of Dallas Willard in

The Spirit of the Disciplines are particularly helpful here, most especially his emphasis on training, not trying.[14] We don't run a successful marathon, or learn to play the piano, or grow in our discipleship or our leadership abilities, simply by trying harder: the idea is ridiculous. It is only through a serious training programme—a commitment, in our spiritual lives, to 'train yourself to be godly' (1 Timothy 4:7)—that we can truly grow in our ability to be led by Christ and to lead like him.

Confident leadership: the tale of two gardens

As we witness the demise of Goliath, and David's subsequent withdrawal from the scene to allow the Israelites and their officers a slice of the action, I am reminded of two spectacular gardens I have visited recently. The first surrounds Hampton Court Palace, the former home of Cardinal Wolsey, Henry VIII and many subsequent kings and queens of England, and is largely laid out in a formal French style, with every tree cut exactly to shape and every plant geometrically positioned to create a well-ordered and symmetrical effect. The second adjoins the Palladian mansion of Stourhead in Wiltshire, and is a paradise of lakes and woods and temples and vistas, English landscape gardening at its spectacular best.

Both gardens include both the natural and the artificial: Henry Hoare, who created Stourhead, was just as passionate about the need for garden design and the careful positioning of trees and shrubs as his opposite number at Hampton Court. Both gardens reflect extraordinary creativity and dogged hard work. But while the formal garden requires a constant shaping of trees and cutting of branches to maintain the symmetry of the whole, the landscape garden allows those trees to grow in their natural shape and to their fullest height. There is a kind of 'humility' about the whole Stourhead enterprise, amid the confidence of its execution—a sense that once a tree or shrub has been planted, it is allowed to grow with minimal interference by gardeners who know when to stop.

It's only a rough analogy, of course, but perhaps the Hampton Court garden expresses Level 4 leadership, while Stourhead reaches the heights of Level 5. The bravado and charisma of the designer of the formal gardens is indisputable, conveyed in every clipped tree and elaborate flowerbed. Plants will thrive in such an environment, provided they are the right kind of plants—preferably not too large and able to be shaped at will. But the landscape garden involves a quite different approach on the part of its designer: an overriding vision, yes, but also a willingness to 'play to the strengths' of the trees and combine those strengths to spectacular effect. Some will walk round such a garden without giving any thought to its designer: it's the trees themselves and the vistas that take your breath away. Others will assume that the garden is virtually unplanned and will flourish on its own, without recognising the time and energy which went into damming the river and planting the woodland, the vision which even now is creating a new vista here, a fresh planting there.

And while your average board of directors and interview panel will continue to be dazzled by the Level 4 leader, the key question is whether or not such leaders aspire to Level 5: whether their vision, ambition and motivation lead ultimately to the goal of personal fame and fortune, or to the building up of a great company (or family, institution, church or nation). Two scriptures are especially relevant here: the first, Jesus' call to us to 'seek first [God's] kingdom and his righteousness' (Matthew 6:33); the second, Peter's challenge to 'humble yourselves… under God's mighty hand, that he may lift you up in due time' (1 Peter 5:6). And the wise interviewer, looking to employ a confidence-imparting leader, could do far worse than to ask themself the questions, 'How are they doing in the humility stakes?' and 'Whose kingdom are they seeking?'

— 9 —

Confidence at the Coalface:
David and Saul

It was Tony Blair who remarked that while being Prime Minister was sometimes 'a tough job', being a parent was 'probably tougher'. One of his children had been on a drinking spree to celebrate the end of his GCSE exams, and had ended up at Charing Cross police station, where he'd lied about his name, address and age. There was censure from some quarters as a result, but the prevailing response was one of deepest sympathy. Certainly few parents of teenage children felt justified in throwing the first stone!

And there's something about that incident which encapsulates the theme of this chapter: the question of how we can walk with confidence in the midst of our ordinary living, and especially in those difficult times when we are let down (even opposed) by those who should be on our side. When there's a major external threat hanging over a family or community, a church or nation, it is possible to discover a sense of solidarity, a unity of purpose which overrides our petty squabbles and enables us to proceed with courage and a sureness of step. In that sense, Goliath served a useful purpose for his opponents, acting as a focus for unity in a more effective way than King Saul (or even King David) ever could. But what happens when Goliath is struck down and beheaded? What happens when the euphoria of VE Day comes to an end, only to be replaced by the dreary reality of ration books, coal shortages and devaluations of the pound? No one in their right mind would want the war to continue, but how much more difficult it is to walk with confidence and togetherness when the big external threat has passed.

It's an issue raised in a number of the Bible narratives, not simply in the story of David and Goliath. The book of Nehemiah, for example, ends not with a celebration of the fulfilment of Nehemiah's vision to rebuild the Jerusalem wall, but with the hero returning to the city some years on, only to find that very little has really changed. There's a heroism about Nehemiah earlier in the story when he's inspiring God's people to complete the work in the face of the taunts and threats of their opponents; but there's not much that's heroic about Nehemiah 13, where the mighty wall-builder is reduced to rebuking people, calling down curses on them and pulling out their hair (v. 25). Had the book finished with the massed choirs and orchestras of the previous chapter, it might have been a more satisfying read (for by and large we like our stories to start 'once upon a time' and end 'they all lived happily ever after'), yet the Bible doesn't encourage such superficial thinking. Instead it forces us to confront the reality of confidence in the mundane; of walking with a sureness of step whether we're dealing with lofty affairs of church and state or with a teenager who has just returned from a party the worse for wear; of responding appropriately to the many disappointments that life throws at us, and especially to the opposition of those who should really be our friends.

And so to the aftermath of the battle: a meeting between Saul and David which (in any decent fairy tale) would have been the icing on the cake, with the young shepherd boy congratulated, cheered to the rafters and covered with wealth and honours in the build-up to a lavish royal wedding. In a subsequent chapter we read of Jonathan's defence of his friend before his father: 'He took his life in his hands when he killed the Philistine. The Lord won a great victory for all Israel, and you saw it and were glad' (19:5). But any sense of gladness that Saul may have felt at the death of the Philistine giant was immediately replaced by other darker emotions, and the result was a meeting characterised not so much by warmth and celebration as by coldness and formality. There was to be no 'happily ever after' so far as David and Saul were concerned.

A frosty encounter

As Saul watched David going out to meet the Philistine, he said to Abner, commander of the army, 'Abner, whose son is that young man?'

Abner replied, 'As surely as you live, Your Majesty, I don't know.'

The king said, 'Find out whose son this young man is.'

As soon as David returned from killing the Philistine, Abner took him and brought him before Saul, with David still holding the Philistine's head.

'Whose son are you, young man?' Saul asked him.

David said, 'I am the son of your servant Jesse of Bethlehem.'

1 SAMUEL 17:55–58

It's a question which David asked on more than one occasion: 'What will be done for the man who kills this Philistine and removes this disgrace from Israel?' (vv. 26, 30); and each time the answer was the same. 'The king will give great wealth to the man who kills him. He will also give him his daughter in

marriage and will exempt his family line from taxes in Israel'
(v. 25).

In the event, though, the promised reward proved little
more than a cruel hoax. There is no indication that Saul
endowed David with 'great wealth' in the aftermath of the
fight—indeed, the subsequent chase through the desert
reduced the young shepherd boy to a state of near penury.[1]
Nor is there any further mention of tax breaks for David's
family: instead, both his parents and brothers were forced
into exile themselves, judging it safer to join David in the
cave of Adullam than to stay at home and brave it out. The
cave—in which David was also joined by 'all those who were
in distress or in debt or discontented'—was soon adjudged
too uncomfortable for David's parents. It's ironic that these
elderly Israelite loyalists were forced to accept the hospitality
of the king of Moab, one of Israel's historic enemies—
although maybe Jesse's own Moabite blood (through his
paternal grandmother Ruth) enabled him to feel rather more
at home in the country than other Israelites would have
done (see 1 Samuel 22:1–4).[2]

It's true that David was temporarily elevated to a high rank
in Saul's army (18:5): indeed, some commentators argue that
David's promotion to the position of an armour-bearer to the
king in 16:21–22 belongs to this post-Goliath period, which
would partially (if not entirely) help to explain the king's
ignorance of David's family background at the end of chapter
17. It's true, too, that he got his girl, tactfully negotiating
a rejection of Saul's older daughter Merab in favour of her
lovely and love-struck sister Michal. But even these apparent
blessings were accompanied with deadly intent on Saul's part.
The Philistine price on David's head would be significantly
higher as the king's son-in-law than as a mere giant-slayer;

and Saul's request for a 'hundred Philistine foreskins' as a bride-price for Michal was as dangerous as it was disgusting (18:24–25).[3]

All this lay in the future, of course. Meanwhile Saul's concern (not least as a potential father-in-law) was to discover a little more about David's family background. Abner, the commander of Saul's army, was duly despatched to greet David straight from the battlefield, and to bring him (Goliath's dripping head in his hands) before the king. It's an image much treasured by Renaissance painters such as Michelangelo, Bernini and Caravaggio, as well as by Dutch artists Rembrandt and Jacob van Oost the Elder, but it seems to have evoked nothing from the lips of Saul. 'Whose son are you, young man?' asked the king. 'I am the son of your servant Jesse from Bethlehem,' replied the giant-killer; and that was that.

There's not much to be added about the content of this exchange, beyond the simple observation that David emphasised the loyalty of his father as the king's 'servant'. But it's the chilly atmosphere of the encounter—soon to be exacerbated by the tactless singing from David's fan club (18:7)—which sets the mood for the whole of the rest of 1 Samuel. In chapter 17 David purposefully refrained from using the name of Goliath, instead referring to him as 'the uncircumcised Philistine' or 'this disgrace'; in subsequent chapters Saul starts to do the same with the name of the shepherd boy, increasingly replacing the word 'David' with the phrase 'the son of Jesse' or even 'my enemy' (20:27–31; 22:7–9; 19:17). In chapter 17 the animal imagery—lions, bears, dogs and birds—largely centred on Goliath; in subsequent chapters it is David who feels like a dead dog, a flea and a hunted partridge (24:14; 26:20).

Within the dim recesses of Saul's paranoid ego, there remained a need for Public Enemy Number One. And now that the post had been unexpectedly vacated through the death of the Philistine giant, who better to fill it than a man whose sheer charisma, courage and white-hot faith played into every conceivable insecurity of a deeply troubled mind?

This was not to prove David's darkest hour—that dubious accolade was to be awarded to an incident later in his life (and following the Bathsheba fiasco), when it was David's son Absalom, not the king, who was hunting him down (see 2 Samuel 15). Yet whether it be paranoid monarchs or rebellious children, colleagues or fellow believers, family members or those among our closest circle of friends, there is nothing more dispiriting than to be let down, even opposed, by those who should be on our side. In that sense, the Goliath times are the easy times, while it's the subsequent infighting which inflicts by far the greatest damage on families, communities, churches and nations. 'Where would you prefer to live and minister—East or West Germany?' I once asked a Dresden pastor whose family was then facing continual harassment from the Communist state authorities. 'The east,' he replied, 'because at least we know who our enemy is.'

The call to improvise

In Chapter 6, I used the analogy of the jazz band to help explain the need to play to our strengths without simply repeating the same old melody time and again; and there's something improvisatory about David's behaviour in the later chapters of 1 Samuel, ducking and diving to keep one step ahead of the king. Sometimes the improvisation paid off brilliantly: on two occasions, for example, he had Saul at his mercy but refused to take advantage of the situation, thus earning himself a temporary reprieve from the king's hatred (chapters 24 and 26). At other times the improvisation was a near-disaster: David's brazen decision to offer himself as a mercenary to the king of Gath (though with no intention of fighting against his own people) proved to be the most extreme of extreme sports (chapters 27 and 29). In the duel with Goliath, the courage and confidence required were considerable, but at least it was clear what David had to do. In this new situation there were no clear rules, historic precedents or even guidelines to follow: before young David came along, no Israelite had ever been hunted down by his own king.

This element of improvisation, of having to duck and dive, is well known to many a parent, especially a parent of a teenage child. It is quite possible to be bombarded with half a dozen requests from the child in the course of a single conversation, and to have to sift out the good from the bad from the downright dangerous at record speed and (all too often) with much of the relevant information deliberately withheld. With a more rebellious young person, the requests may well be accompanied with a barely concealed element of threat ('I'm going anyway, so what are you going to do about it?'), and with an ever-decreasing list of effective sanctions at the parent's disposal. In such situations, even those with the power to take their country into war or secure a hostile takeover of a rival business empire are likely to be seriously wrong-footed, unless their improvisatory skills are honed to a remarkable degree.

The same applies where conflict breaks out in a small community, perhaps a school. The head teacher may be quite used to dealing with budgetary threats from the local authority, and to winning over a potentially sceptical parent body to the changes she deems necessary. But it's that whisper of insubordination from within—that sense, perhaps, that the deputy is getting too big for his boots—which is far more difficult to deal with. Is it the head's own paranoia that is giving credence to the whispers, or are they true? What level of support does her deputy have among the teaching staff, and how does that compare with her own position in the staff's affections? Is a quiet word with the deputy all that's needed, or should she institute a more formal disciplinary hearing? Might even the quiet word backfire, giving fuel to the argument that the head is simply jealous of her deputy's superior gifts and people-skills?

Churches are not immune from such divisions—far from it. On a local level, the careful manoeuvring to keep both organist and band-leader happy (or to negotiate a peaceful resolution to a surprisingly vicious dispute that has erupted within the flower team) sometimes occupies a disproportionate amount of the church leader's time; on a broader canvas, issues of gender and sexuality threaten to tear whole denominations to shreds. In the face of external threats—the decision by a local council to drop all mention of Christmas in its yuletide celebrations—the church's response will generally be strong and united. But once the threat is past (or at least perceived to be so), maintaining the unity of the Spirit can be a whole lot more challenging.

But is improvisation in such situations really a polite word for guesswork, for doing the first thing that comes into our heads? Or are there any principles which might guide us along the way, giving us a background rhythm and harmonic structure against which our improvisation should be set?

Reading the account of David's wilderness years in the second half of 1 Samuel helps to draw out three commitments which were fundamental to David's sanity over this period: commitment to God, to his king, and to the king's son Jonathan. Standing in faith, living in integrity and drawing on friendship were key values for David at this point; and the same is true for us if we are to tread a similarly hazardous path with any kind of surefootedness and assurance.

Standing in faith: a continuing commitment to God

As David first faced the full blast of Saul's jealousy in 1 Samuel 19, it is interesting that his immediate reaction was to seek out Samuel the prophet, and that his subsequent itinerary took in the sanctuary at Nob. In both cases his motivation was a mixed one: he was probably safer by Samuel's side than on his own, and the priests at Nob provided food for his men, alongside a formidable piece of weaponry (21:1–9).[4] But there's also a sense in which David needed holy people at this point, those who would encourage his faith in the Lord who had called and anointed him. The wilderness years would prove a time when David's faith was profoundly shaken; but somehow he came through that time with his faith intact, even strengthened.

It wasn't simply the presence of holy men that helped David during this period. With his reputation as a worshipper, as 'Israel's singer of songs' (2 Samuel 23:1, NIV), there's little doubt that his commitment to personal prayer and worship was seriously sustaining too. In the book of Psalms there are 73 psalms that are attributed to David; 14 of those psalms carry headings which connect them to events in his career, while eight of the 14 relate specifically to this wilderness period, as Saul chased him around the Judean desert.[5] The historical value of these ascriptions has been treated with scepticism by many commentators, sometimes with good cause;[6] but more recently there have been others, notably Brevard Childs, who have demonstrated that the links between the titles and the poems have rather more significance than is often acknowledged.[7]

The wilderness psalms are full of expressions of a continuing faithfulness to God in the midst of the darkest of situations: 'The Lord is my rock, my fortress and my deliverer... I called to the Lord, who is worthy of praise, and I have been saved from my enemies' (Psalm 18:2–3); 'The Lord is close to the broken-hearted and saves those who are crushed in spirit' (34:18); 'My heart, O God, is steadfast, my heart is steadfast; I will sing and make music. Awake, my soul! Awake, harp and lyre! I will awaken the dawn' (57:7–8). The image of David cheerfully 'awakening the dawn' with harp in hand—leading the whole of creation in morning worship—is an attractive one at the best of times; yet how much more impressive a commitment it shows when set against the backdrop of Saul's murderous intentions.

Holding on to God in the wilderness—and especially where we are opposed by those who should be on our side—is inevitably a challenging exercise, a 'sacrifice of praise', in that telling phrase from the letter to the Hebrews (13:15). In another of the psalms attributed to David, we read how 'even my close friend, someone I trusted, one who shared my bread, has lifted up his heel against me' (Psalm 41:9); and the pathos of those words is matched in the New Testament where John writes of Judas' speedy exit from the breaking of the bread at the last supper (13:26–30), and where Mark writes of Jesus' disciples, 'They all forsook him, and fled' (14:50, RSV). In such circumstances, how easy to lose any sense of God's presence at all, as famously expressed in another of the psalms of David: 'My God, my God, why have you forsaken me?' (22:1).

Whatever the sense of temporary abandonment, though, the importance of maintaining our spiritual bearings in the wilderness cannot be stressed too highly. For some, that will require a new discipline in their spiritual lives—perhaps a move towards a structured form of praying rooted in the scriptures and the traditions of the church,[8] rather than something more piecemeal and subjective. For others, it will require regular trips to spiritual directors and Christian communities, much as David sought out Samuel and the priests at Nob to 'enquire of the Lord' on his behalf (see 1 Samuel 22:10, 15). Christian couples and prayer partners should make the most of every opportunity to pray together, to seek the Spirit's guidance and to read the scriptures— especially drawing on the (often embattled) spirituality of the Psalms, of Paul's epistles[9] and of the letter to the Hebrews. Personal prayer should include times of worship and thanksgiving alongside honest and heartfelt cries for help.

How do we tread confidently through the wilderness? 'It is God who arms me with strength,' writes David, 'and keeps my way secure' (Psalm 18:32).

Living in integrity: a continuing commitment to Saul

We might expect God to play a fairly key role in David's thinking as the shepherd-boy ducked and dived in the desert; but more surprising perhaps is the young man's continuing loyalty to the king. Saul, by this point, had become little short of a monster, a man driven by the most powerful and deadly of demons. Yet David consistently referred to him as 'the Lord's anointed' (see 1 Samuel 24:6; 26:9), he was conscience-stricken after cutting off a corner of Saul's robe (24:5), and on at least two occasions he had Saul's life in his hands but resolutely resisted the temptation to kill him (24:4; 26:8–9). When a young Amalekite came to report Saul's death in the battle of Gilboa, he embellished the story, no doubt expecting David to reward him richly for his alleged part in the king's downfall. Instead David asked him, 'Why weren't you afraid to lift your hand to destroy the Lord's anointed?' and had him put to death (2 Samuel 1:1–16); and the ensuing lament for Saul and Jonathan—with its famous cry, 'How are the mighty fallen!' (1:19, RSV)—could hardly have been more genuine and heartfelt.

David's loyalty to the king was not accompanied by any sense that Saul's conduct was explicable, or that he, David, was somehow in the wrong. Whenever the shepherd-boy appeared before Saul he resolutely protested his innocence, and several of the wilderness psalms pick up this integrity theme (for example, 18:20–24). Instead, David's loyalty was based on a clear sense that Saul had been anointed by God, and that there were to be no shortcuts in David's own rise to the kingship. Loyalty can go too far, of course, when it involves carrying out the dishonest or unjust orders of our superiors, but that was not the case here; and at a time when loyalty is in short supply—when the wisdom and actions and motivation of others (most especially those in authority) are frequently judged in the harshest of lights—David's continuing commitment to his king in the face of severe provocations is both instructive and inspiring.

A continuing loyalty to our children, our parents, our partners, our fellow believers, our erstwhile friends and colleagues can be extraordinarily difficult in the context of strained relationships, disappointed expectations, rejection or betrayal. It's far easier, in the short term at least, to revert to the well-trodden paths of gossip, slander, division and bitterness, whether or not we feel personally culpable in the situation which faces us. But there's something about keeping our own integrity intact, about holding on to our moral (as well as our spiritual) bearings, about learning to forgive 'seventy times seven' (Matthew 18:22) and not to allow a 'bitter root' to grow within us (Hebrews 12:15), which is fundamental to our psychological well-being during the wilderness years. We may need professional help (even a place of safety) in cases where the situation is getting out of hand: the call to loyalty must never become an abuser's charter. But the casual belittling of other people—the snide remark thrown out both widely and indiscriminately—is simply not worthy of the children of God.

Parents in Pain is the title of one of John White's most helpful books (IVP, 1979), informed by decades of experience in a private psychiatric practice. Amid much practical wisdom is an encouragement to replace one question, 'How can I rear my children successfully?' with another, 'How can I become a good parent?' 'The first question,' as he puts it, 'is concerned with results. It enquires about success, and by success it wants to be assured that the process of child-rearing will produce a certain kind of child. The second question leaves the matter of results open. The first question focuses on what parents can do, the second on what we should be' (p. 21).

There are times (in White's experience) when disaster strikes, frequently in the form of a severe teenage rebellion, with all the feelings of anger, impotence and shame that can entail on the part of the parents. 'Hitting the ceiling,' he writes, 'is only the start.'

> *It is being scraped down; landing on the hard floor; slowly putting pieces of yourself together again; getting creakingly to your feet and beginning to walk (there is no choice: you have to go on): it is in doing all this that the pain begins. And it must all be done without laying the pain and resentment on your family—most especially on the child who has caused you hurt. They know they've hurt you. You need not, you must not grind their faces into the dirt. (pp. 61–62)*

White is writing in a specific context, of course, but there is something universal about his final sentence. David never ground Saul's face into the dirt: his approach was much closer to that of Jesus, whose appeal 'Father, forgive them, for they do not know what they are doing' (Luke 23:34) remains one of the most inspirational prayers of all time. And 'your attitude,' writes Paul, 'should be the same as that of Christ Jesus' (Philippians 2:5, NIV).

Drawing on friendship: a continuing commitment to Jonathan

Amid the jealousy, compromise, hatred and murder which tarnish the latter chapters of 1 Samuel, there is one relationship characterised by warmth, intimacy, faithfulness and mutual support: the friendship between David and Saul's son Jonathan. Theirs was not, I think, a sexual union: the David story reveals its hero as hot-bloodedly heterosexual, sometimes dangerously so; but it was a friendship of the closest kind, and something of a political alliance too.

Certainly Jonathan's action in giving David his robe and his armour (gifts which the shepherd-boy had previously refused from Saul) suggests that the king's son was willing to relinquish his own claim to the throne in favour of David the giant-killer (1 Samuel 18:4).

The language of covenant—and the Hebrew word *hesed*, which speaks of covenantal loyalty—is used on several occasions to describe the committed relationship that existed between the two men. In 1 Samuel 18, Jonathan 'made a covenant with David because he loved him as himself' (v. 3), and this commitment was renewed on two later occasions (20:16; 23:18) as Saul's paranoid behaviour made both David's and Jonathan's position more and more insecure. Perhaps the most moving verse in this whole section relates to the second of those covenant renewal ceremonies, when David was at his lowest: 'While David was at Horesh', we read, 'he learned that Saul had come out to take his life. And Saul's son Jonathan went to David at Horesh and helped him to find strength in God' (23:15–16). It's a wonderful description of godly friendship—helping the other find strength in God—and the fact that Jonathan was provided at just this point is a strong indication of the Lord's continuing blessing on the shepherd-boy even during a particularly difficult and alarming period of his life.

In *The Four Loves*, C.S. Lewis writes of the low value which the contemporary world places on the gift of friendship when compared to its significant place within the classical and biblical traditions. 'To the Ancients,' he writes, 'Friendship seemed the happiest and most fully human of all the loves; the crown of life and the school of virtue. The modern world, in comparison, ignores it.'[10] Lewis traces some of the reasons for the change, most notably the rise of the Romantic movement, with its tendency to devalue all relationships outside the exclusive and sexually charged. But the rediscovery of this gift—the need for individuals and nuclear families to seek companionship outside the four walls of their homes as well as within them—is an important corrective to the Romantic vision, especially during our wilderness times.

'It is not good for the man to be alone', was God's judgement as he looked at Adam in the Garden of Eden (Genesis 2:18); and there are times too when 'it is not good for the nuclear family to be alone'. Faced with the challenge of a terrible toddler or a trying teenager—grasping the nettle of a difficult relationship within our workplace, community or church—even the strongest of couples can struggle to support one another without some wider friendship-base to offer prayer, counsel and practical help. Perhaps that is part of the purpose of our wilderness times. They act as a humbling reminder that self-sufficiency (and even a self-sufficient marriage) was never God's intention for humanity.

I am delighted to belong to a group of nine clergy who have met together every May for (at the time of writing) the past 29 years. Over a 48-hour period, each of us has a leisurely opportunity to communicate what has been happening over the past year and to pray for one another—a great privilege in the midst of busy and frequently challenging ministries and family situations. There are some years when I've valued our time together in a somewhat superficial way; there are others when I've really needed it. And that group is the closest I come to covenant friendship—a long-term commitment to one another to meet, to share, to pray.[11] It is also a reflection of Jonathan's calling in 1 Samuel 23: for amid the laughter and the tears, the games of croquet and the prayer, our vision when we meet together is to 'help [one another] to find strength in God'.

Ducking and diving

It would be entirely wrong to suggest an easy answer to the problems that this chapter raises, or to imply that a particular recipe will produce a successful result again and again. A raging Saul is both frightening and unpredictable, and the same may become true of those we work with and worship with, those we parent and those we befriend. Any reading of the latter chapters of 1 Samuel will quickly reveal the difficult choices forced upon David, and (at times) the wrong decisions he made as a result. But the simple observation that he came through this period in one piece—the very fact that his spiritual, moral and relational bearings remained intact through the toughest of trials—is a testimony to the strength of his character, the faithfulness of his friends and the ongoing presence of his God.

In the words of one of the wilderness psalms: 'As for God, his way is perfect: the Lord's word is flawless; he shields all who take refuge in him' (Psalm 18:30).

— Conclusion —

The Confident Christian

Her situation looked completely hopeless. Here she was, a married woman caught making love to a man who was not her husband. It was not simply embarrassing or shameful, it was downright dangerous: for under the law of the day she could be stoned to death, and those who had caught her were demanding nothing less. And as she crouched there, waiting in terror for the inevitable, some words cut across the angry condemnation of the crowd, a sentence spoken with unusual calmness and authority: 'Let any one of you who is without sin be the first to throw a stone at her.' There was silence for a few seconds; then a few embarrassed murmurs; then the sound of shuffling feet as, one by one, her accusers left.

Just one person remained, the only man who was truly 'without sin'—the one who had the right to throw that first stone. 'Woman, where are they?' he said. 'Has no one condemned you?' 'No one, sir', she replied. 'Then neither do I condemn you,' said the man. 'Go now and leave your life of sin' (John 8:3–11).

Resurrection confidence

It is that sense of amazed relief that lies at the heart of one of the most glorious passages in the whole Bible, the last section of Romans 8. For the rhetorical passion which led young David to throw out the defiant question, 'Who is this uncircumcised Philistine, that he should defy the armies of the living God?' was clearly inherited by Paul; and towards the end of Romans 8 he throws out no fewer than seven questions of his own.

In my last congregation I had a woman who insisted on answering the rhetorical questions which start to pepper *my* sermons whenever they reach a certain spiritual altitude. It was an annoying habit, but one which no doubt kept me humble! And were that woman to sit through a reading of this passage, her answer to most of Paul's questions would be identical.

'If God is for us, who can be against us?' The answer: 'No one.' 'Who will bring any charge against those whom God has chosen?' The answer: 'No one.' 'Who then can condemn?' The answer: 'No one.' 'Who shall separate us from the love of Christ?' The answer: 'No one.' (See Romans 8:31, 33–35.)

'Woman, where are they? Has no one condemned you?' 'No one, sir,' she replied.

So what of the one person who is left behind when all the others have sheepishly wandered away, the one man who has every right to throw the first stone? Paul describes exactly what he is doing: 'Christ Jesus', he says, 'who died— more than that, who was raised to life—is at the right hand of God and is also interceding for us' (v. 34). He is not interceding against us. He is not calling for the full penalty of the law to rain down on our heads. He is interceding *for* us; and 'if God is for us', we repeat (as the altitude increases), 'Who can be against us?' 'No one,' my former congregation member correctly, if annoyingly, responds!

Romans 8 is the culmination of a long line of argument which spells out the grounds of our Christian hope and confidence. Jesus is first introduced as a 'descendant of David' in his earthly life and as one 'who through the Spirit of holiness was appointed the Son of God in power by his resurrection from the dead' (1:3–4). David is mentioned; so is the resurrection; and already we sense that the 'living God' is at work!

But this is to be no exercise in shallow optimism or wishful thinking, for while Paul is clearly committed to the first part of the Stockdale Paradox, the 'faith that you will prevail in the end', he is equally committed to its second part, the 'discipline to confront the most brutal facts of your current reality, whatever they might be' (see Chapter 2). It's a discipline played out in the early chapters of Romans through the themes of humanity's sin and powerlessness, God's wrath and judgement; and the emphasis is not on some external Goliath juggernaut, but rather on the moral compromise of those facing the threat.

Paul could have brought in the devil at this point (as he does in 16:20) or spoken of the 'spiritual forces of evil' (as he does in Ephesians 6:12) or written of death itself as 'the last enemy' (as he does in 1 Corinthians 15:26). The apostle could have given us a lurid picture of Satan as the ultimate Goliath, and of the deadly armies at his disposal. But the brutal fact that Paul is seeking to convey here is that we only have ourselves to blame—that 'all have sinned and fall short of the glory of God' (3:23), thus reducing us to the status of 'God's enemies' (5:10). And any attempt to wriggle out of that responsibility, by Jew or Gentile alike, is just as inappropriate as the series of evasive answers which so derailed the reign of Saul the king.[1]

'It is not by sword or spear that the Lord saves,' asserted David (1 Samuel 17:47), and his subversive statement lies at the heart of Jesus' arrival on the scene. Those who assumed that the true 'Goliath' was the hated Roman Empire, and who witnessed Jesus cleansing the temple of God rather than marching on the palace of Pilate, were horribly confused. Those who expected that the Messiah would be a military hero were bitterly disappointed. Instead the Son of David appeared on the scene, both speaking and acting with authority, but making no attempt to reach for weaponry. Rather, he was captured by 'Goliath' and brutally put to death.

So how is Paul 'not ashamed' of this gospel (Romans 1:16)? What kind of 'gospel' is it anyway? The answer lies in Jesus' resurrection, an event so momentous in its implications that, following the appearance of the risen Christ to Paul himself, the apostle chose to take three years out, no doubt practising the prayer of *examen* (see Chapter 1) and rebuilding his faith from its very foundations (see Galatians 1:17–18). The letter to the Romans is sprinkled with references to the resurrection and to the 'sacrifice of atonement' (3:25) which preceded it. Through Christ's death and resurrection, both Jew and Gentile can know and experience peace—not the temporary ceasefire from our human enemies which David secured, but an eternal peace with God himself.

This gospel story should not have been entirely unexpected for those who had seen the 'movie trailers' provided in the Law and the Prophets (see Romans 1:2, 3:21), but it could not, and cannot, be neatly reconciled with human reasoning because through it 'the righteousness of God is revealed' (1:17), and reason and revelation always make unlikely bedfellows (see Chapter 2). Another trailer in the Old Testament, the story of Abraham, demonstrates how peace with God is to be secured—not through circumcision, the Law or our human efforts, but through a faith which was 'credited to him as righteousness' (Romans 4:9; Genesis 15:6)—while David makes his second appearance in Paul's letter in a quotation from Psalm 32 which stresses 'the blessedness of those to whom God credits righteousness apart from works' (Romans 4:6–8). Faith is central to this whole enterprise: God calls us to be people with faith (in the Latin, *con fides*). And the heart of this confidence is neither our CV (outlining our extraordinary achievements) nor the list of referees who are willing to speak up on our behalf. It is rather 'amazing grace', the entirely unmerited love of God.

In 1 Samuel 17 the Israelite army could have watched impassively as David defeated Goliath, then gone back home again. They could have failed to make any connection between David and themselves, and so remained enslaved by fear and compromise. And the same is true of the Christian: it would be possible (in theory at least) to put our faith in Christ and remain wholly unchanged, even to decide to 'go on sinning, so that grace may increase' (Romans 6:1). In reality, David's victory both motivated and liberated God's people to rediscover joy, faith and courage, and a confidence to win many victories of their own; and in the same way, writes Paul, the triumph of Christ has set us free from our former paralysis and slavery,[2] so that we can live in new freedom and righteousness, joyfully counting ourselves 'dead to sin but alive to God in Christ Jesus' (6:11).

And so we come to chapter 8—a passage which is brutally honest about the 'groaning' of creation, of God's people and even of the Spirit of God himself, but which consistently places those groans in the context of the maternity unit, not the hospice (see 8:22–27). That cheerful setting is a surprise, since Christians are *dying* in this chapter: Paul, quoting from another of the Psalms, writes that 'for your sake we face death all day long; we are considered as sheep to be slaughtered' (v. 36; Psalm 44:22). Yet Jesus has died and risen again, and so it will be for all who die 'in Christ', indeed for the whole of God's creation. It is the powerful events of the first Good Friday and Easter Day which enable Paul to write that 'in all things God works for the good of those who love him, who have been called according to his purpose' (Romans 8:28), the most comprehensive statement of the providence of God in the whole of scripture.

Thus we return to Paul's rhetorical questions at the end of chapter 8, and to a confidence which is as glorious as it is secure. 'I am convinced,' writes Paul, 'that neither death nor life, neither angels nor demons, neither the present nor the future, nor any powers, neither height nor depth, nor anything else in all creation, will be able to separate us from the love of God that is in Christ Jesus our Lord' (vv. 38–39).

Tom Wright, reflecting on this passage, writes with an inspiring rhetoric of his own:

Look what the Messiah has done, and is still doing even as we speak. Look around and see the many things that threaten to separate you from the powerful love which reaches out through the cross and resurrection, and learn that they are all beaten foes. Learn to dance and sing for joy to celebrate the victory of God. The end of Romans 8 deserves to be written in letters of fire on the living tablets of our hearts.[3]

Life confidence

If this gospel marks the beginning of the pilgrim's progress and the foundation of the Christian's confidence, how do we proceed and build on that foundation? Again Paul picks up many of the themes we have already explored in the David and Goliath narrative.

First—in relation to his own ministry—there is a clear sense that Paul knew what he was called to be, that he had discovered the 'big Yes' which should guide and direct his steps (see Chapter 6). Just as David's vocation was as a 'shepherd of his people Jacob, of Israel his inheritance' (Psalm 78:71), so Paul was called to be an 'apostle, set apart for the gospel of God' (Romans 1:1). This ministry came with a more specific brief 'to call all the Gentiles to faith and obedience for [Jesus'] name's sake' (v. 5) and 'to preach the gospel where Christ is not known' so as to avoid 'building on someone else's foundation' (15:20). It made Paul 'eager to preach...in Rome', the very heart of Gentile power and influence (1:15), and led him to include the distant Spain on a future itinerary (15:24). And it's unquestionably this defining vision which enabled the apostle to resist a more settled style of ministry and to reject the 'armour' of other people's pastoral and ministerial expectations: as he put it elsewhere, 'Christ did not send me to baptise, but to preach the gospel' (1 Corinthians 1:17).

It's fruitful for leaders to specialise, as Paul discovered, but it's only possible if there are others who are prepared to work alongside them, exercising complementary specialisms of their own; and there are real indications that the church in Rome had embraced this vision. Right from the outset of the letter, Paul stressed that the church as a whole was 'loved by God and called to be his holy people' (1:7); a moment later he wrote of his desire to impart to them 'some spiritual gift to make you strong', then checked himself and added, 'that you and I may be mutually encouraged by each other's faith' (1:11–12).

That sense of mutuality underlies much of the rest of the letter, and especially Paul's familiar image of the body of Christ in chapter 12: 'in Christ we, though many, form one body, and each member belongs to all the others. We have different gifts, according to the grace given to each of us' (vv. 5–6). In Romans 16, he gives a long and moving list of some of his fellow workers, women and men, who had variously 'been the benefactor of many people', 'risked their lives for me', 'worked very hard for you', 'been in prison with me', 'worked very hard in the Lord' and 'been a mother to me'. There is absolutely no indication of a division between those who 'do' ministry and those to whom it is 'done'; and that fact alone would account for the vibrancy of a church whose faith was 'being reported all over the world' (1:8).

What kind of leadership can release this dynamic energy among the people of God? As we have seen, a 'Level 5' leadership fits the bill, characterised by 'extreme personal humility' and an 'intense professional will'. Paul's (like David's) was an unusual form of humility, and not one characterised by a sense of diffidence or indecision. Yet Paul's willingness to be a 'servant of Christ Jesus' (Romans 1:1), a servant of the gospel (Ephesians 3:7) and a servant of the church (2 Corinthians 4:5) was exemplary, expressing itself in dogged hard work and an extraordinary capacity to endure opposition, ridicule, flogging, imprisonment and even death for the sake of Christ and his people. 'Never be lacking in zeal,' he urged others, too, 'but keep your spiritual fervour, serving the Lord' (Romans 12:11).

When compared with the false apostles in Corinth, there is no question of Paul's selfless Level 5 credentials. In brief, the false apostles were show horses, while the true apostle was a plough horse (see 2 Corinthians 11).

And the key to Paul's continuing commitment to a vision larger than himself was a life of great discipline and a daily decision to live in the power of God's Spirit. As he puts it in Romans 8:12–14:

Therefore, brothers and sisters, we have an obligation—but it is not to the sinful nature, to live according to it. For if you live according to the sinful nature, you will die; but if by the Spirit you put to death the misdeeds of the body, you will live. For those who are led by the Spirit of God are the children of God.

How did Paul and the Christians in Rome go about their gospel ministry? In Chapter 7, I described the early church's commitment to proclaiming Christ by word and deed, and roughly equated the various 'weapons' they used with the fivefold ministry of apostle, prophet, evangelist, pastor and teacher—and all five approaches are alluded to in Paul's letter to the Romans. The courageous willingness to embrace (even rejoice in) our sufferings without complaint or retaliation (5:3–5, 12:17); the role of miraculous 'signs and wonders' in the proclamation of the gospel (15:18–19); the evangelical commitment to personal transformation (12:1–2); the sacrificial love within the community (12:9–10; 15:25–27); the blessing of 'truthful speech' to educate and inspire (10:14–15)—all have their place in this letter, and all should play their part in the ministry and mission of the church today. Were the church of Christ to be characterised by courage, spiritual power, transformed priorities, sincere love and gracious truth-telling, the gospel stories emerging from that church would be inspiring and profound.

And what, finally, of confidence at the coalface? How did Paul cope with the everyday struggles and privations of his unusually demanding ministry, especially when confronted with the opposition of those who should have been his allies? Taking a leaf out of David's book, he did so in three ways: through a continuing commitment to God (most poetically expressed in the beautiful doxology at the end of Romans 11); through a continuing commitment to his friends (as demonstrated in the loving warmth of chapter 16); and through a remarkable and enduring loyalty to those who opposed him, especially his enemies within the Jewish community.

'Saul, Saul, why do you persecute me?' had been the question put to him by Jesus as Paul made his way to Damascus to hunt for followers of the Way, arrest them and have them put to death (Acts 9:4). (Exactly the same question might well have been uttered by David a thousand years before as he too was hunted down by an earlier Saul, with arrest and execution clearly on the king's agenda.) And perhaps it was Paul's dual experience as persecutor and persecuted that gave him a unique insight into this area. 'Bless those who persecute you; bless and do not curse' (Romans 12:14), as he put it; 'Do not take revenge, my dear friends, but leave room for God's wrath' (v. 19); 'Do not be overcome by evil, but overcome evil with good' (v. 21).

Towards the end of his letter, Paul asked for the church at Rome to 'pray that I may be kept safe from the unbelievers in Judea' (15:31). It's clear that he sensed real danger as he planned to revisit Jerusalem. A little earlier on he spoke of these Jewish unbelievers as enemies of the gospel (11:28). But regardless of that, and in spite of the floggings he'd endured at their hands (see 2 Corinthians 11:24), he was adamant that Israel was chosen by God, loved by God, special to God. In fact, Paul's 'sorrow and unceasing anguish' on behalf of Israel—his willingness even to be 'cursed and cut

off from Christ for the sake of my people' (Romans 9:2–3)—
is just as impressive as David's enduring commitment to King
Saul, the 'Lord's anointed', and his heartfelt anguish at the
king's death.

Overcoming the siren voices

Towards the end of Romans 16, Paul comforts his readers
with the striking promise that 'the God of peace will soon
crush Satan under your feet' (v. 20). It's an image very close
to that of the battlefield at the Valley of Elah, and it raises
the question of how that can be—how individual Christians
and their leaders, churches and their denominations, can live
with the kind of proactive confidence that leaves the giant
floored, and his unholy spiritual cohorts 'strewn along the
Shaaraim road to Gath and Ekron' (1 Samuel 17:52).

In earlier chapters I have referred on occasion to Homer's
The Iliad; but perhaps this question is best answered with
reference to its sequel *The Odyssey*[4]—for in that epic we read
of the sirens—bird-like creatures, but with women's heads
and lions' claws—whose song was so ravishing that many
boats were shipwrecked on their shores. Odysseus duly
ordered his men to put wax in their ears, so as to deafen
them to the song of the sirens; and he had himself firmly tied
to the mast of the boat, so he could hear the song but not
steer the ship into danger.

In another classic text, though—*The Argonautica*[5] by
Apollonius Rhodius—we are told of a second approach to the
seduction of the sirens—the strategy of Orpheus, the most
famous musician and poet of ancient times. As the Argonauts
approached the sirens' island, Orpheus didn't reach for the
wax and the rope. Instead he took up his lyre and started to

sing an even more ravishing song than the song of the sirens; and so the boat passed safely through.

And that is the Christian challenge today. The songs of the society around us—its increasingly secular mantras about material affluence, sexual rights, privatised faith and the choice of a made-to-measure lifestyle in a world where there is no objective right and wrong—are deeply seductive songs. They also lead to shipwreck after shipwreck. But the Church's calling is not to fill our ears with wax, or to tie ourselves (or others) to the mast. It is rather to pick up our lyres with confidence, and sing a more beautiful, life-giving song, the glorious melody of the gospel of a Christ whose service is perfect freedom.

Discussion Guide

Where this book is used in a small group setting, it is important that members read the relevant chapter in the days before the group is due to meet. This may well raise issues for discussion, into which these suggested questions, additional Bible passages and prayer suggestions can be incorporated.

Introduction: The Call to Confidence (2 Timothy 1:3–7)

1. If God has given us a spirit of 'power, love and self-discipline', how might you 'fan into flame' this gift of God within you? (2 Timothy 1:6–7).
2. How easy do you find it to place your confidence in God in your daily living? How does that confidence (or lack of it) express itself?
3. In what else are you tempted to place your confidence?
4. When do you feel at your most self-confident—and when at your least? Is there such a thing as godly self-confidence, and if so, what might it look like?
5. What is the difference between confidence and triumphalism, and how can the church grow in one without drifting into the other?
6. 'It is perhaps that sense of confidence as a verb which leads many to be drawn more to the story of courageous individuals than to the abstract reflections of the philosopher or theologian' (p. 14). Whose such stories have been an inspiration to you?

7. The letter to the Hebrews contains several references to the theme of confidence (3:14; 4:14–16; 10:19–22; 10:35; 13:5–6). Take a few minutes to read these through and reflect on them—then turn these verses into a prayer that you would grow in faith and trust in the living God.

Chapter 1: Building Confident Foundations (1 Samuel 17:1–3)

1. Do you tend to be a reflective person, or do you focus more on the present and future? How might you make more time to learn from your successes and failures?
2. If you could pass on just one lesson from your Christian story, what would that lesson be? What has been the most life-changing event of your life so far?
3. The book of Deuteronomy is all about the need to remember—to learn from both the happy and the unhappy lessons from Israel's past (for example, 5:15; 7:17–18; 8:2–3; 9:7; 11:18–21). Why was it so important that the Israelites remembered these things as they prepared to enter the promised land? Do some of those verses connect with your own experience of life and faith and God?
4. The Bible can also talk about the need to forget things—to put them right behind us (for example, Isaiah 43:18–19; Philippians 3:13–14). When do you think is the right time to do that, and how is it possible?
5. Looking back at the history of your family (or your church), are you aware of any repeating patterns (positive or negative) contained within that history? How might you benefit from the strengths of your spiritual inheritance, while avoiding its potential pitfalls?

6. At the end of Chapter 1, there are four lessons drawn from the history of Israel's previous dealings with the Philistines. How might attending to those lessons build up your godly confidence?

7. The five-stage approach to the prayer of *examen* is one that many people have found helpful. Take a few minutes to reflect (quietly or aloud) on the past day, using the Jesuit practice as your model.

Chapter 2: Confidence, Faith and Wishful Thinking (1 Samuel 17:4–10)

1. 'You must never confuse faith that you will prevail in the end—which you cannot afford to lose—with the discipline to confront the most brutal facts of your current reality, whatever they might be.' Which part of the Stockdale Paradox do you find it most difficult to hold on to? Should Christians be optimists or pessimists?

2. Why is wishful thinking so attractive—and such a mistake?

3. What are the Goliaths you face in your workplace or family, your church or your personal life?

4. How might they place you on the back foot and paralyse you, preventing you from living as a confident Christian believer?

5. What are the chinks in the armour of our modern-day Goliaths?

6. When have you been most aware of the spiritual dimension of the battles you face (see Ephesians 6:10–12; 1 Peter 5:8–9)? How does that awareness affect the way you think and act and pray?

7. The 'full armour of God' in Ephesians 6 is a powerful image of both the protection and the weaponry we have

at our disposal. As you take time to reflect on some of your personal Goliaths, read Ephesians 6:10–18 and prayerfully 'put on' the full armour of God, committing yourself to the same practice each day of the coming week.

Chapter 3: Confidence within God's Church (1 Samuel 17:11)

1. R. Paul Stevens writes of two categories of people: those who 'do' ministry and those to whom it is 'done'. How far does your church life reflect that description, and how might the church more fully embrace the 'priesthood of all believers'?
2. Most people are employed to do a good job of work, and not to be ministers or missionaries. How can we honour Christ in a secular workplace without abusing the trust of those for whom we work? (1 Thessalonians 4:11–12 and 1 Peter 2:12 might be helpful here.)
3. How should godly leadership (in the church and outside) differ from the leadership of the 'Gentiles' who 'lord it over' others (Matthew 20:25)? How far do we believe that we get the leaders that we pray for—and what effect should that have on our prayer life?
4. The story of Saul reminds us how compromise robs us of our spiritual authority. How does that happen, and what are the conditions on which spiritual authority can be restored?
5. What might your church look like if the gifts and visions of its members were truly unleashed?
6. What's the leash?
7. 1 Corinthians 12 includes the vision of the church as the body of Christ. Reflectively read through verses 12–31,

then take some time to pray for your church, that every member would find a fruitful and fulfilling place within it.

Chapter 4: Confidence in the Providence of God (1 Samuel 17: 12–27)

1. What are the attractions of deism, and why does it easily become the default setting for a church that has lost its way?
2. At what time of your life have you been most aware of the presence of the 'living God'? Are there ways in which we could practise the presence of God more fruitfully?
3. If you were to give a testimony of God's providence over the past seven days, what would you focus on?
4. The Israelite army had been in the same place for nearly six weeks; David was a newcomer on the scene. Why can it be important to listen to the first impressions of newcomers to our churches, workplaces and homes?
5. In the apartheid era, Desmond Tutu prayed, 'For goodness' sake, why don't You make it more obvious that *You are* in charge?' How can we hold on to the doctrine of God's providence during times of pain, grief, persecution and injustice?
6. Is there a new perspective that might cut our 'Goliaths' down to size?
7. 1 Peter 1:3–9 combines a realism about the Goliaths that surround us with a powerful sense of the providence of God and his future plans for his people. Read it aloud, then praise God for the glorious truths that lie at its heart.

Chapter 5: Responding to Godly Confidence (1 Samuel 17:28–37)

1. Reflecting on David's courage, what is your attitude to risk in God's service? What from your upbringing has contributed to that attitude?
2. Have you ever been in the position of David in this passage, where your enthusiasm has been met with indifference or hostility? How did you respond to that setback?
3. When did you last sense the 'Eliab reaction' in yourself? What triggered it?
4. How do you relate to Saul in this passage? Are there times when you have been tempted to write someone off but have later been relieved that you resisted the temptation?
5. Being excluded from his sister's party became a defining image in Frank's life. Do you relate to that image—or are there other incidents which have permanently shaped the way you look at yourself and the world around you?
6. David is a key figure in the Old Testament and Peter in the New. Why does God place such a high premium on faith?
7. Psalm 133 focuses on the themes of unity, blessing and life, and the images of anointing oil and refreshing dew. Meditate on the psalm and pray for a growing ability to listen, not to prejudge, and a new commitment to live in unity with those around you.

Chapter 6: A Right Self-Confidence (1 Samuel 17:38–40)

1. The 'big Yes' in David's life was his call to be a shepherd. How clear are you of the 'big Yes' in your life—and how might you seek to clarify it further?

2. 'When I run, I feel his pleasure,' says Eric Liddell in the film *Chariots of Fire*. Can you think of a time when you have felt the pleasure of God?

3. When did you last sense that you were being squeezed into the armour of other people's expectations? What did it feel like? Did you escape?

4. Are there times when we should conform to the expectations of others—and when might they be?

5. 'There is a need for others to articulate our strengths for us, rather than assuming... that we're already fully conscious of where they lie.' What holds people back from articulating the gifts and strengths of others? Could we start to do that today?

6. In what sense (if any) do we feel ourselves 'anointed' by God for the roles which we now exercise? How might that sense of anointing free us to be the people whom God is calling us to be (see 2 Corinthians 3:17)?

7. 2 Corinthians 1:21–22 speaks of how God anoints us with his Spirit, enabling us to stand firm in Christ. Reflect on these verses, then pray for a fresh touch of God's Spirit to strengthen you, release you and equip you for the week ahead.

Chapter 7: Confidence in Sharing the Gospel (1 Samuel 17:41–47)

1. Goliath had a way with words, a talent which he used to belittle his opponents. Have there been times when others have tried to belittle you—and if so, what have you found to be the best response?

2. In view of Paul's teaching in Romans 12:14 (and James' teaching in James 3:1–11), how can you tame your own

tongue, especially in the face of mockery and provocation?

3. When have you witnessed evangelism at its most fruitful? What were the key factors which contributed to its success?

4. The latter part of Chapter 7 lists five evangelistic 'weapons' at the Christian's disposal, which roughly correspond with the calling of the apostle, prophet, evangelist, pastor and teacher. With which of these weapons are you most familiar—and how might you grow in your calling to be a Christian witness, without being squeezed into a particular evangelistic mould?

5. 'Her time in [the hospice] completely changed the outlook of many people who worked there: many people came into her room and left inspired.' How might the way we choose to embrace suffering become an inspiration to those without faith?

6. 'The battle is the Lord's.' What impact might this make on the way you face the challenges of the coming week?

7. In 2 Corinthians 4 Paul speaks of the 'light of the knowledge of God's glory displayed in the face of Christ' (v. 6)—a vision that he himself had witnessed on the road to Damascus. He also refers to Christians as 'jars of clay' (v. 7) in which this gospel treasure is deposited. The themes of light and darkness, life and death, encouragement and perplexity all form part of Paul's experience as a preacher and evangelist. Read through this passage, then pray that the God might inspire you afresh both to be good news and to speak good news to those around you.

Chapter 8: Confidence-Imparting Leadership
(1 Samuel 17:48–54)

1. Who has been the best leader under whom you have lived and worked? How have their leadership qualities compared with those of the 'Level 5' leader?

2. How do you respond to Harry Truman's maxim, 'You can accomplish anything in life, provided you do not mind who gets the credit'? Why is personal humility such an important quality in excellent leadership?

3. 'He was more of a show horse, whereas I was more of a plough horse,' wrote one Level 5 leader. What is the place of hard work in the Christian life, and how does this relate to the much-trumpeted 'work–life balance'?

4. How might it look if we were genuinely to 'seek first God's kingdom and his righteousness' (Matthew 6:33)? What might be the next step towards us doing that?

5. Both David and Jesus were filled with the Spirit and practised in the spiritual disciplines. How might we grow in these attributes, which are fundamental to our development as Christ-like leaders and disciples?

6. To which garden are we instinctively drawn—Stourhead or Hampton Court? How (if at all) does that reflect the kind of leadership under which we like to work?

7. John 13:1–17 reflects both Jesus' 'extreme personal humility' and his 'intense professional will'. Take time to read the story and to reflect on the leadership which you are currently called to exercise, praying that you might be shaped by the example of Christ. Pray too for God's grace on any you know who carry considerable leadership responsibility.

Chapter 9: Confidence at the Coalface (1 Samuel 17:55–58)

1. Why might it sometimes be tougher to be a parent than a prime minister?

2. What is the most significant area of your life in which you feel the need to 'duck and dive'? Does it feel like improvisation or blind guesswork?

3. 'There is nothing more dispiriting than to be let down, even opposed, by those who should be on our side.' How have you experienced that in your own life, and what has been your response?

4. What are the resources that enable us to hold on to God in the wilderness times? Are there any fresh resources that you need to access today?

5. How is it possible to remain committed to those who give us a tough time, without giving way to bitterness or feelings of revenge? How does the example of Jesus help us in this respect (see 1 Peter 4:12–14)?

6. What priority are you giving to friendship at the moment? How might you help a friend 'to find strength in the Lord'?

7. The superscription to Psalm 56 relates it to a particularly dangerous time in David's wilderness years. Read the psalm and reflect on its rapidly changing emotions. Bring to God those times in which you've felt the same, and pray for renewed trust in times of fear and danger.

Conclusion: The Confident Christian (Romans 8:31–39)

1. When have you been most aware of God's 'amazing grace'? How can we avoid a deadening overfamiliarity with the gospel story?

2. Why does Paul spend so much time dwelling on the bad news before he moves on to the good news? What are the dangers of a theology which sidesteps the themes of 'humanity's sin and powerlessness, God's wrath and judgement'?

3. What does the resurrection mean to you? How can we 'learn to dance and sing for joy to celebrate the victory of God'?

4. Faith is sometimes seen as a commodity, something we either 'have' or 'don't have'. How would you respond to someone who said, 'I'd like to have faith, but I just don't have it'? Can people learn to put their faith in God even while they struggle with doubts about his existence?

5. How can the church sing a more beautiful song than the world around it? How might our own church grow in its attractiveness to those who are not yet Christians?

6. The section on 'Life confidence' summarises some of the big themes of the book as a whole. What is the single most important insight you've gained from your reading—and what are you going to do about it?

7. Pray about the areas that you have identified in question 6; then finish by reading Romans 8:31–39 aloud (without answering the rhetorical questions!), praying that these words would be 'written in letters of fire on the living tablets of our hearts'.

Notes

Introduction

1 This incident is also recorded in 2 Chronicles 32 and Isaiah 36.

2 See John Bunyan, *The Pilgrim's Progress*, first published in 1678.

3 We will spend some time considering Paul's letter to the Romans in the conclusion of this book.

4 For more on narrative theology, its strengths and drawbacks, see Alister McGrath, *Christian Theology: an Introduction* (Blackwell, 2001), pp. 167–170.

5 *Joseph and the Amazing Technicolor Dreamcoat* continues to pull in the crowds nearly 50 years after it was first produced.

6 Bruce C. Birch in *The New Interpreters Bible*, Volume 2 (Abingdon Press, 1998), p. 1114.

7 Walter Brueggemann, *David's Truth in Israel's Imagination and Memory* (Fortress Press, 1985), p. 31.

8 Bruce C. Birch (*The New Interpreter's Bible*, p. 1108) refers to the work of Robert Alter, and especially to *The Art of Biblical Narrative* (Basic Books, 1981), pp. 150–151.

9 His most accessible commentary is *First and Second Samuel* in the series *Interpretation: a Bible Commentary for Teaching and Preaching* (John Knox Press, 1990).

10 Brueggemann, *First and Second Samuel*, p. 1.

11 We will be returning to the work of Dawkins (author of *The God Delusion*) and Hitchens (author of *God Is Not Great*) in future chapters.

12 A line from the hymn 'Hail to the Lord's Anointed', written by James Montgomery in 1821. The reference, of course, is to Jesus.

13 There is a rough correlation here between the right and left eyes in my metaphor and the division of the brain into a creative right side and a more analytical left side.

14 Chapter 1 is the only partial exception to this 'rule'.

Chapter 1: Building Confident Foundations

1 'History Lesson' from *Poems: The Best of Steve Turner* (Lion, 2002). First published in *Up to Date* (Hodder, 1983). Copyright © Steve Turner. Used with permission.

2 I am grateful to the Bishop of London for suggesting this illustration in a sermon to the clergy of his diocese.

3 Desmond Tutu, *No Future Without Forgiveness* (Rider, 1999). The brief quotations are all from chapter 2, pp. 10–36.

4 I am delighted to add that our conversation persuaded the couple to take this issue seriously, and that their marriage is going swimmingly!

5 A quotation from the Collect for the second Sunday of Advent in the Book of Common Prayer.

6 The list of the inhabitants of the promised land in Exodus 3:8.

7 Clara Wieck, who went on to become Schumann's wife, famously called Wagner's opera *Tristan and Isolde* 'the most disgusting thing I have ever seen or heard in my life'.

8 Schumann's legacy lives on in those who are happy with the church as a provider of high culture, but are far more negative when the church goes into mission mode.

9 Gaza is the one Philistine city which remains untouched, primarily because of the ongoing political tensions in the region.

10 Neal Bierling wrote up his researches in *Giving Goliath His Due: New Archaeological Light on the Philistines* (Marco Polo monographs 7, Shangri-La Publications, 2002), also available free on the internet: www.phoenixdatasystems.com/goliath/contents.htm.

11 *The Iliad* was probably written in the seventh or eighth century BC and, along with its companion piece *The Odyssey*, forms one of the earliest and most impressive works of literature in the classical world. The role of Homer in writing the epics, or in distilling centuries of oral tradition, has been widely debated, as has the historicity of the Trojan War itself. The apparent discovery of Troy by the German archaeologist Heinrich Schliemann in 1870 has led to fresh thinking on this

score, with most scholars arguing for some historical basis to the epics, though interlaid with much which is plainly mythical. Among various translations of *The Iliad*, the most famous is that by E.V. Rieu, published by Penguin Classics (revised edition 2003).

12 Sixty per cent of the nearly 400 references to Philistines in the Bible are to be found in the books of Samuel, when this policy of expansion was largely taking place.

13 His wife Timnah, a prostitute from Gaza in chapter 16 and, of course, Delilah.

14 The Philistines know about the Exodus story in 1 Samuel 4:7–8, even though they hadn't quite got a grip on the fierce monotheism of their opponents.

15 Although note the reference to Melchizedek, king of 'Salem', in Genesis 14:18.

16 Richard Foster informs us that '*Examen* comes from the Latin and refers to the weight indicator, or a balance scale, hence conveying the idea of an accurate assessment of the true situation' (Foster, *Prayer: Finding the Heart's True Home*, Hodder & Stoughton, 1992, p. 27). See also Fr. Timothy Gallagher, *The Examen Prayer* (Crossroad Publishing, 2006).

17 In many ways the Twelve Steps of the Alcoholics Anonymous Programme represent a similar approach to reflection, confession and accountability.

Chapter 2: Confidence, Faith and Wishful Thinking

1 Jim Collins, *Good to Great* (Random House, 2001), pp. 83–85.

2 See Robert Gordon, *1 and 2 Samuel: A Commentary* (Paternoster Press, 1983), p. 154.

3 See H.W. Hertzberg, *I and II Samuel* (SCM Press, 1964), p. 148.

4 Robert Pershing Wadlow (1918–40) currently holds that accolade in *The Guinness Book of Records*, coming in at an impressive 8 foot 11 inches.

5 The Masoteric text (MT) dates back to the third century BC, but has long been considered rather unsatisfactory when it

comes to parts of the books of Samuel. The Septuagint (LXX) was a Greek translation of the Old Testament, also begun in the third century BC by order of the Egyptian Pharaoh Ptolemy II. The Dead Sea Scrolls consist of 900 documents, discovered in eleven caves between 1947 and 1956. Three Hebrew scrolls of the books of Samuel were found in Cave 4 (generally known to scholars as 4QSam), which are often closer to the Septuagint than the Masoteric text.

6 Bierling (*Giving Goliath His Due*) suggests that this word should rather be translated 'scimitar'.

7 Note the reference to the Philistines' iron-making abilities in Chapter 2.

8 Homer, *The Iliad* (in the translation by E.V. Rieu), Book 3, lines 330–40.

9 *The Iliad*, Books 11 and 18.

10 The only other biblical reference to a similar event is found in 2 Samuel 2:14–16.

11 *The Iliad*, Book 3, lines 87 and following.

12 Winston Churchill, *The Hinge of Fate* (Houghton Mifflin, 1986) p. 54. *The Hinge of Fate* was the fourth volume of Churchill's war memoirs, covering the year 1942.

13 My grandmother's memoirs were written up in the Chinnor church magazine from 1983 to 1988, and privately published under the title *Dr Mary*.

14 Dawkins, *The God Delusion*, p. 31. For concise reflections on *The God Delusion* see Mike Starkey, *Whose Delusion?* (Grove Books, 2007).

15 *Proper Confidence*, p. 17.

16 Ali wrote a book with this title in 1976.

17 Released in 2006, the film won an Oscar and is currently the third highest-grossing documentary ever made.

18 The earliest of these books was published by Brierley's previous organisation MARC Europe, the latter three by its successor Christian Research. *The Tide Is Running Out* and *Pulling Out of the Nosedive* are reflections on the English Church Censuses of 1999 and 2005.

19 See Bob Jackson, *Hope for the Church* (CHP, 2002) and *The Road to Growth* (CHP, 2005).

Chapter 3: Confidence within God's Church

1 Available in Penguin Classics (1998).
2 We might compare the Greeks' response to the challenge of Hector in *The Iliad*: 'So [Hector] spoke and was received in complete silence by them all. They were ashamed to refuse his challenge, but afraid to accept it. Eventually Menelaus rose to his feet and, saddened at heart, reproached them bitterly: "What does this mean, you big mouths, you women?"' (Book 7, line 93).
3 Brueggemann, *First and Second Samuel*, p .57.
4 See 1 Samuel 9:16; 10:1, where the Hebrew word is *nagid* (leader, captain), not *melek* (king).
5 See 10:27, where these so-called 'troublemakers' may have disapproved of Saul himself, or have been motivated by more ideological concerns about kingship. There is evidence in these chapters that the compiler has brought together material from a number of sources, some of them more positive to Saul than others.
6 This song employed classic Hebrew parallelism, and was probably placing Saul and David in the same category rather than implying that David was superior (compare Psalm 91:7; 144:13; Micah 6:7). It is repeated several times in 1 Samuel, suggesting that it became something of a popular hit. We find a group of women tactlessly singing it in Saul's presence in 18:7, Saul ruminating over it in 18:8; the servants of Achish (king of Gath) referring to it in 21:11; and the Philistine commanders mentioning it in 29:5. In Psalm 3, attributed to David, the psalmist writes, 'I will not fear though tens of thousands assail me on every side' (v. 6).
7 The command to destroy everything in the wake of the Amalekite defeat is problematic in today's context, although we can better understand the principle that Saul and his men should not have profited personally from the battle. For more

on this theme and the way it plays out in the book of Joshua, see John Wenham, *The Goodness of God* (IVP, 1974), chapter 8.

8   The phrase 'an evil spirit from the Lord' in this verse is difficult. The author of the book of Samuel is not willing to drift into an easy dualism which portrays God on one side and Satan on the other; instead he recognises that evil spirits are ultimately subject to God's control and, more widely, that Saul's mental disorder has spiritual roots in the king's increasing alienation from God.

9   R. Paul Stevens, *The Other Six Days* (Eerdmans, 2000), p. 3 (first published under the title *The Abolition of the Laity* in 1999).

10 1 Peter 2:9 and three references in the book of Revelation (1:6; 5:10; 20:6); see also the foundations of the doctrine in Exodus 19:6.

11 Stevens, *The Other Six Days*, chapter 2.

12 For more on Jesus' views of leadership, see Andrew Watson, *The Fourfold Leadership of Jesus* (BRF, 2008).

13 Stevens, *The Other Six Days*, p. 171.

14 The full series was as follows: 'Work: blessing or curse?' (Genesis 1—2); 'Work: meaninglessness or satisfaction?' (Ecclesiastes 1:17–26); 'In authority, under authority' (Colossians 3:22—4:1); 'The prudent student' (Proverbs 1:1–7); 'Success and failure' (Luke 10:17–20; John 6:60–69); 'Integrity in the workplace' (Luke 7:1–10); 'Is ambition a sin?' (Mark 10:35–45; 1 Timothy 3:1–13); 'Evangelism in the workplace' (Luke 5:1–11, 27–32); 'Coping with the pressure' (Matthew 11:25–30); 'Retirement: waiting for God?' (Luke 2:25–38); 'How to rest when the work is never done' (Exodus 20:8–11); 'God's workmanship' (Ephesians 2:1–10). 'Work' was defined in as broad a way as possible.

15 See Frank Tillapaugh's excellent book on this subject, *Unleashing the Church: Getting People Out of the Fortress and into Ministry* (Regal Books, 1985).

16 See Acts 2:17–18, a fulfilment of Joel 2:28–29. See also Moses' 'dream' in Numbers 11:29: 'I wish that all the Lord's people were prophets and that the Lord would put his Spirit on them!'

Chapter 4: Confidence in the Providence of God

1 Grace Davie, *Religion in Britain since 1945* (Blackwell, 1994).

2 J.B. Phillips, *Your God Is Too Small* (first published by Wyvern Books, 1952); John Young, *Our God Is Still Too Small* (Hodders, 1988); Bruce Ware, *Their God Is Too Small* (Crossway, 2003). 'Open theism' broadly teaches that God can only speculate regarding what the future holds.

3 This according to the Mishnah, which laid down that a priest could not offer incense more than once in a lifetime; some priests never received this privilege (*Tamid* 5:2).

4 See Hertzberg, *I and II Samuel*, pp. 146–148 for a fuller discussion of the various differences between the Masoteric text and the Septuagint. The shorter Septuagint text goes directly from verse 11 to verse 31.

5 I am grateful to Max Lucado for this insight: *Facing Your Giants* (Nelson, 2006), p.16.

6 This was a particularly important lesson in view of the previous (and ultimately disastrous) appointment of King Saul, someone who himself is described as 'an impressive young man without equal among the Israelites—a head taller than any of the others' (1 Samuel 9:2, NIV).

7 Gordon, *1 and 2 Samuel*, p. 155. There is a third interesting possibility—that the (comparatively) private anointing of David, his empowering by the Spirit of God and his subsequent victory over Goliath correspond to a similar process in Saul's somewhat elaborate coronation as king.

8 'It is tempting to find here a contrast between David, so eager for battle he checks things in the baggage department, and Saul, who preferred to hide in the baggage' (Brueggemann, *First and Second Samuel*, p. 128).

9 Kirk Bottomley, 'Confessions of an Evangelical Deist' in Grieg and Springer (eds.), *The Kingdom and the Power* (Regal, 1993), p. 259.

10 Harvey Cox, *Fire from Heaven* (Addison Wesley Longman, 1994).

11 Alister McGrath, *The Twilight of Atheism* (Random House, 2004), p. 197.

12 Saul did have a later 'Pentecostal' encounter on his way to capturing David in 1 Samuel 19:23–24, though no one, I suspect, was more surprised about it than Saul himself.

13 I contributed a number of these to John Woolmer's book *Encounters* (Monarch, 2007), which collects several such stories from among John's friends and colleagues.

14 In Part 2 of Charles Taylor's *A Secular Age* (Harvard, 2007), the author traces the development of this providential deism as a step on the path towards full secularisation.

15 Julian of Norwich, *The Revelations of Divine Love* (Penguin Classics, 1998). Julian was born in 1342, and had a series of intense visions during a time of severe sickness in her early 30s.

16 Kathryn Tanner, 'Creation and Providence' in *The Cambridge Companion to Karl Barth* (CUP, 2000), p. 125. We will return to this theme in the conclusion.

17 Tutu, *No Future without Forgiveness*, p. 2.

Chapter 5: Responding to Godly Confidence

1 See R.A. Knox, *Enthusiasm* (OUP, 1950), p. 450.

2 I am delighted to have served in an area of the London Diocese which had the following in its mission statement: 'Our vision… is of a church confident in the faith where worshipping communities… take responsibility for ministry and mission. It is of a church where the values of the kingdom of God and worship in the power of the Spirit transform both individuals and society.'

3 Jesus' 'brothers' were technically half-brothers or even (as has been suggested) step-brothers.

4 Interestingly, this famous phrase comes before David arrives on the scene—just as the words 'You are my Son, whom I love; with you I am well pleased' (Luke 3:22) occur before Jesus begins his ministry in the Galilean countryside.

5 For a further development of this theme, see Watson, *The Fourfold Leadership of Jesus* (pp. 62–66).

6 See Jackson, *The Road to Growth*, especially pp. 21–24, 113–123.

7 Chapter 3 explores the nature of the duel in *The Iliad*, and might suggest that Saul would have kept on fighting even if David had lost the battle: so this may not have been quite as all-or-nothing a situation as it appears.

8 Henri Nouwen, *The Return of the Prodigal Son* (DLT, 1994).

Chapter 6: A Right Self-Confidence

1 Sally Magnusson, *The Flying Scotsman* (Quartet, 1981), p. 30.

2 See *The Iliad*, especially Book 3, lines 329–339, where Paris prepares for his duel against Menelaus.

3 *The Iliad*, Book 16.

4 Gordon, *1 and 2 Samuel*, p. 157.

5 As Walter Brueggemann puts it, 'David's contrast is with both Saul and Goliath. Unlike them, he goes unencumbered ("I am not used to them"). Both of them—the one a braggard, the other a coward—trust in arms' (*David's Truth in Israel's Imagination and Memory*, Fortress, 1985, p. 33).

6 Stephen Covey mentions the 'big Yes' in his bestseller *The Seven Habits of Highly Effective People* (Simon & Schuster, 1994).

7 See www.gallup.com; also the helpful book by Marcus Buckingham and Donald O. Clifton, *Now, Discover Your Strengths* (Simon & Schuster, 2002).

8 See, for example, Rick Warren's teaching about our SHAPE in *A Purpose-Driven Life* (Zondervan, 2002), chapters 30—32, where SHAPE stands for Spiritual Gifts, Heart's desire, Abilities, Personality and Experience; Buckingham and Clifton, *Now, Discover your Strengths*, which includes a very helpful internet-based Strengthsfinder profile, allowing readers to discover their five core strengths; James Lawrence, *Growing Leaders* (BRF, 2004), especially chapter 5.

Chapter 7: Confidence in Sharing the Gospel

1 *The Iliad*, Book 13, p. 238. Hector could be just as abusive to those on his own side, calling Paris a 'sex-crazed seducer'.

2 Dawkins, *The God Delusion*, p. 31.

3 See Watson, *The Fourfold Leadership of Jesus*, especially Part 3, for further thoughts about Jesus' ministry and that of the Zealots, who advocated armed resistance against Rome.

4 See, for example, Hector in his abuse of Paris, and Elijah in his condemnation of Ahab and Jezebel: 'Dogs will eat those belonging to Ahab who die in the city, and the birds will feed on those who die in the country' (1 Kings 21:24). See also Jeremiah 8:1–3 and 16:6, verses which illustrate the Israelites' horror at the prospect of not receiving a proper burial.

5 See Shelby Foote, *The Civil War, A Narrative: Red River to Appomattox* (Random House, 1974). Sedgwick was a Union Army general in the American Civil War.

6 This phrase can also be translated 'the Lord of hosts' (which makes its canonical debut in 1 Samuel 1:3). The hosts may include angelic beings alongside the physical army of Israel.

7 'Epistle to Diognetus' section 7, published in *Early Christian Writings* (Penguin, 1968), p. 179. The epistle was probably written around AD 124.

8 Augustine, *The City of God*, Book 22, chapters 8—10, translated by H. Bettenson (Penguin, 1984). The evangelistic impact of healing and exorcisms is a regular theme in earlier Christian apologetics, from the New Testament itself through to Origen, Justin and Tertullian.

9 See www.uk.alpha.org

10 Chapters 22 and 26; also see Galatians 1:11f.

11 Justin Martyr, 'First Apology 14' (*The Ante-Nicene Fathers*, Volume 1, Cosimo, 2007). It could be that Paul was talking about this kind of Christian integrity when he wrote of the 'weapons of righteousness' in 2 Corinthians 6:7, although some commentators interpret the phrase as a reference to the gospel message itself, through which the righteousness of God is revealed (see Romans 1:16–17).

12 Michael Green, *Evangelism in the Early Church* (Hodder & Stoughton, 1970), p. 181.

13 Tertullian, 'Apologeticus 39', published in H. Bettenson, *Early Christian Fathers* (OUP, 1969), p. 142. Tertullian lived from around AD 160 to 225, and was a church leader in Carthage.

14 For helpful reflections on this theme, see the article 'Revival Time?' by Jim Wallis in *Third Way* magazine, April 2008.

15 Eusebius, *Historia Ecclesiastica* 6.3.

16 Gregory Thaumaturgus, *Panegyric on Origen*, section 6.

Chapter 8: Confidence-Imparting Leadership

1 Collins, *Good to Great*, p. 18.

2 Collins, *Good to Great*, p. 31.

3 In Collins' hierarchy, Level 1 leaders are highly capable individuals, while those at Level 2 are contributing team members. Level 3 leaders are competent managers, and Level 4 effective and charismatic individuals with a clear and compelling vision. Level 5 leadership is at the top of the tree.

4 For further reflections on this theme, see John Adair, *The Leadership of Jesus* (Canterbury Press, 2001), chapter 10.

5 *The Iliad* (Penguin, revised translation 2003), p. xxxiv.

6 Compare also the Benjamites in 1 Chronicles 12:2, who 'were able to shoot arrows or to sling stones right-handed or left-handed'.

7 This situation would be temporarily reversed at the end of 1 Samuel, where Saul's head was cut off and his armour placed as a trophy in the temple of the Ashtoreths (31:9–10). For now, though, Israel was in the ascendancy.

8 Shortly afterwards, David went to Goliath's home town of Gath, where he formed a brief and ambivalent alliance with King Achish, a measure of the young man's desperation at that point (see Chapter 9).

9 Hertzberg (*1 and 2 Samuel*, p. 153) notes that no one has even come up with a satisfactory origin for the name 'Golgotha', and postulates the idea of the rock formation. *Golgotha* is an Aramaic word, while the Latin for 'skull' is *calvaria*, from

which we derive the word 'Calvary'. For Gospel references to Golgotha, see Mark 15:22; John 19:17.

10 1 Chronicles 20:4–8 lists several giant-killers among David's men, including Jonathan, son of Shimea, who killed a 'huge man with six fingers on each hand and six toes on each foot'. The passage also seeks to clear up an odd verse in 2 Samuel 21:19, which names Elhanan the Bethlehemite as the killer of Goliath the Gittite. Some have identified David with Elhanan, while others have claimed that David's antagonist in 1 Samuel 17 must have been someone other than Goliath. 1 Chronicles 20:5 comes up with a neater solution, which indicates a small scribal error in the 2 Samuel passage.

11 All of Jesus' responses were quotations from Deuteronomy 6 and 8, where God, through Moses, was addressing Israel during her 40 years in the desert and calling the nation to a wholehearted allegiance to him. I have developed this theme in *The Way of the Desert* (BRF, 2009).

12 See also the parallels in Matthew 4:1–11 and Luke 4:1–13.

13 See Matthew 19:28: 'Jesus said to them, "Truly I tell you, at the renewal of all things, when the Son of Man sits on his glorious throne, you who have followed me will also sit on twelve thrones, judging the twelve tribes of Israel."'

14 Dallas Willard, *The Spirit of the Disciplines* (Harper, 1991). See also John Ortberg, *The Life You've Always Wanted* (Zondervan, 2004), which the author describes as 'Dallas for Dummies'. Donald Whitney and Richard Foster have also written wisely on this subject.

Chapter 9: Confidence at the Coalface

1 See his pathetic request for bread in 1 Samuel 21:3.

2 See too the lovely book of Ruth, which tells the story of Jesse's paternal grandparents and how they met.

3 1 Samuel 25:44 also states that Saul 'had given his daughter Michal, David's wife, to Paltiel son of Laish, who was from Gallim'—an illegal act which again demonstrates the state of his paranoia at that point.

4 Goliath's sword had somehow made its way up to Nob in the months (or years) between 1 Samuel 17 and this incident four chapters later. The priests of Nob were later killed for sheltering David in an act which marked the very lowest point of Saul's reign (1 Samuel 22:17–19).

5 Psalms 18; 34; 52; 54; 56; 57; 59; 142. Psalm 18 (on which we will draw in this chapter) purports to be a more reflective poem 'when the Lord delivered [David] from the hand of all his enemies and from the hand of Saul'.

6 Some of the psalms ascribed to David mention the temple, which hadn't been built at the time.

7 B.S. Childs, *Psalm Titles and Midrashic Exegesis*, JSS 16 (1971), pp. 137–150.

8 In the Church of England, this is provided by the various forms of morning and evening prayer in the Book of Common Prayer (1662) and *Common Worship* (2000).

9 2 Corinthians is a particularly powerful letter to read when faced with struggles of this kind.

10 C.S. Lewis, *The Four Loves* (Collins Fount, first published 1960, reprinted 1977), p. 55.

11 The relationship between godparents and the families of their godchildren also fits into the category of a 'covenant friendship'.

Conclusion: The Confident Christian

1 See 1 Samuel 15:12–31 and Chapter 3 of this book for a fuller discussion of this theme.

2 In Romans 8:14–17, Paul also writes of how the Spirit of God has set us free from our 'slavery to fear'.

3 N.T. Wright, *Paul for Everyone: Romans Part 1* (SPCK, 2004), p. 159.

4 Homer, *The Odyssey* (Penguin Classics, revised edition 2003), Book 12.

5 Apollonius, *Jason and the Golden Fleece: The Argonautica* (Oxford World Classics, new edition 1998), Book 4, lines 891–919.

Enjoyed
this book?

Write a review—we'd love to hear what you think.
Email: reviews@brf.org.uk

Keep up to date—receive details of our new books as they happen.
Sign up for email news and select your interest groups at:
www.brfonline.org.uk/findoutmore/

Follow us on Twitter @brfonline

By post—to receive new title information by post (UK only), complete the form below and post to: BRF Mailing Lists, 15 The Chambers, Vineyard, Abingdon, Oxfordshire, OX14 3FE

Your Details
Name _____
Address_____
_____
Town/City _____ Post Code _____
Email _____

Your Interest Groups (*Please tick as appropriate)	
❑ Advent/Lent	❑ Messy Church
❑ Bible Reading & Study	❑ Pastoral
❑ Children's Books	❑ Prayer & Spirituality
❑ Discipleship	❑ Resources for Children's Church
❑ Leadership	❑ Resources for Schools

Support your local bookshop
Ask about their new title information schemes.